378.1662 COM   MAR   2005
Lewis, Rosemary.
Review for the CLEP general
English composition

REVIEW FOR THE CLEP* GENERAL ENGLISH COMPOSITION EXAMINATION

By
Rosemary Lewis, M.A.

This book is correlated to the video tapes produced by
COMEX Systems, Inc., Review for The
CLEP* General English Composition Examination ©1995
they may be obtained from

comex systems, inc.

5 Cold Hill Rd.
Suite 24
Mendham, NJ 07945

KILGORE MEMORIAL LIBRARY YORK, NE 68467

* "CLEP and College Level Examination Program are registered trademarks of College Entrance Examination Board. These Materials have been prepared by Comex Systems, Inc., which bears sole responsibility for their contents."

© Copyright 1978, 1980, 1982, 1984, 1988, 1989, 1992, 1994, 1995, 1996, 1998, 2000, 2001,2003

All rights reserved. No part of this material may be reproduced in any
form without permission in writing from the publisher.

Published by

comex systems, inc.
5 Cold Hill Rd.
Suite 24
Mendham, NJ 07945

ISBN 1-56030-183-X

Table of Contents

CLEP* (College Level Examination Program)

CLEP provides a way to determine the level of knowledge you now have in relation to college level material. CLEP does not determine your ability to learn a subject. People tend to have a low evaluation of their ability. There is no way you can determine your present level unless you take the examination. You can save time and money taking these examinations to earn credit.

WHY DID WE WRITE THIS BOOK?

Our firm has conducted many classroom reviews for CLEP General Examinations. Our instructors have assisted thousands of candidates. From this experience we have determined that:

1. In each area there is specific material beneficial for candidates to know.

2. There is a need for a simple-to-follow review book which helps students improve their ability to achieve.

3. It is important for students to become accustomed to the specific directions found on the examination before taking the examination.

4. It is beneficial to develop a systematic approach to taking an objective examination.

This book will help you perform at your highest potential so that you will receive your best score.

The flyers "CLEP COLLEGES" (Listing where you may take the CLEP tests and the colleges that accept CLEP for credit) and "CLEP INFORMATION FOR CANDIDATES" are available free by calling (800) 257-9558, by writing to: CLEP, PO Box 6600, Princeton, NJ 08541-6600 or online at www.collegeboard.com.

CLEP INFORMATION

WHAT IS CLEP GENERAL?

CLEP is a nation-wide program of testing which began in 1965. Today thousands of colleges recognize CLEP as a way students may earn college credit. Each year hundreds of thousands of students take CLEP examinations. The testing program is based on the theory that "**what** a person knows is more important than **how** he has learned it". All examinations are designed and scored by the College Entrance Examination Board (CEEB). The purpose of each examination is to determine whether your current knowledge in a subject will qualify you for credit in that area at a particular college.

There are five general examinations. The subject areas are:

1. English Composition
2. Mathematics
3. Social Science / History
4. Natural Science
5. Humanities

Credits earned through achieving on these examinations replace basic liberal arts credits which are required by many colleges. Each of these general examinations is very broad in coverage. Questions are from the wide range of subjects included in each of the major disciplines. The General CLEP Humanities Examination will include questions related to literature, music and art. Because of the broad coverage in each examination, you are not expected to be knowledgeable in all areas. There will be some questions on all the tests you will not be able to answer.

HOW LONG ARE THE EXAMINATIONS?

Each CLEP General Examination is 1½ hours in length. Each examination is divided into separate timed portions.

HOW MUCH DO THE EXAMINATIONS COST?

Currently, the fee to take each examination is $50.00. They may be taken one at a time or in any combination. (NOTE: Fees change periodically.)

WHERE WILL THE EXAMINATIONS BE TAKEN?

The CEEB (College Entrance Examination Board) has designated certain schools in each state to serve as test centers for CLEP examinations. The same examinations are given at each test center. If you are a member of the armed forces, consult with the Education Services Officer at your base. Special testings are set up for military personnel. A list of test centers may be found at www.collegeboard.com.

WHEN ARE THE TESTS GIVEN?

Most CLEP examinations are administered during the third week of every month except December and February. The test center chooses the day of the week. A few test centers administer the tests by appointment only. Check with the center where you will take the test for specific information. If you are serving with the United States Military, check with the Education Services Officer at your base to find out about the DANTES testing program. You will be given information about testing as applicable to military personnel.

HOW DO YOU REGISTER FOR AN EXAMINATION?

A standard registration form may be obtained from the test center where you plan to take the examination. Many centers require that you register (send registration form and fee for examinations to be taken) a month prior to your selected date.

WHEN WILL SCORES BE RECEIVED?

Most tests taken on the computer will be scored immediately (the English Composition with Essay must be graded first). If you are in the military and are taking the test on paper it will take up to 6 weeks to receive your scores. You may also request that a copy be sent to a college. The score you receive will be a scaled score. CEEB keeps a record of your scores on file for 20 years. You may obtain an additional copy or have a copy sent to a college if you contact:

College Board
PO BOX 6600
ATTN: Transcript Service
Princeton, NJ 08541
800-257-9558

IS IT NECESSARY TO BE ENROLLED IN A COLLEGE BEFORE YOU TAKE AN EXAMINATION?

Each college has established policies regarding CLEP. Check with the school you wish to attend. Many schools do not require enrollment before taking CLEP examinations.

HOW MANY CREDITS MAY BE EARNED?

Each college determines the number of credits that may be earned by CLEP examinations. Most colleges award six credits for achievement on a CLEP General Examination.

HOW ARE THE EXAMS SCORED?

See page VII for a detailed explanation of scoring.

HOW ARE THE SCORES EVALUATED?

The examinations are administered to college students who are taking a course the examination credits will replace. These students do not take the examination for credit. They take it to establish a standard by which your score will be evaluated. Percentile levels of achievement are determined. For example, if you score at the 25th percentile, this would indicate that you achieved as well as the **bottom** 25 percent of those students who took that examination to set the standard.

There is no correlation between the number of questions you answer correctly and the percentile level you achieve. The number will vary from test to test.

CAN THE SAME SCORES EARN A DIFFERENT NUMBER OF CREDITS AT DIFFERENT SCHOOLS?

Yes, different schools may require different levels of achievement. Your scores may earn more credits at one institution than at another. For example: if you achieve at the 25th percentile level, you could earn credit at a school which required the 25th percentile level; you could not earn credit at a school which required a higher level of achievement.

CAN CLEP CREDITS BE TRANSFERRED?

Yes, provided the school to which you transfer recognizes CLEP as a way to earn credit. Your scores will be evaluated according to the new school's policy.

CAN AN EXAMINATION BE RETAKEN?

Many schools allow you to retake an examination if you did not achieve the first time. Some do not. Check your particular school's policy before you retake an examination. Be realistic, if you almost achieved the level at which you could earn credit, do retake the examination. If your score was quite low, take the course it was designed to replace.

IF YOU DECIDE TO RETAKE AN EXAMINATION, six months must elapse before you do so. Scores on tests repeated earlier than six months will be canceled.

HOW MAY I FIND OUT WHAT SCHOOLS ACCEPT CLEP?

There are many schools that recognize CLEP as a way to earn credit. For a free booklet, <u>CLEP Test Centers and Other Participating Institutions</u>, which lists most of them, send your request, name, and address to:

> The College Board
> Box 1822
> Princeton, NJ 08541
> 800-257-9558
> or check the list at www.collegeboard.com

HOW TO USE THIS BOOK:

Recommended procedure:

1. Complete the review material. Take the short tests included at the end of the lessons.

2. If you do well on the tests, continue. If you do not, review the explanatory information.

3. After completing the review material, take the practice examination at the back of the book. When you take this sample test, try to simulate the test situation as nearly as possible:

   a. Find a quiet spot where you will not be disturbed.

   b. Time yourself accurately.

   c. Practice using the coding system

4. Correct the tests. Determine weaknesses. Go back and review those areas in which you had difficulty.

HOW THE EXAMINATIONS ARE SCORED

There is no penalty for wrong answers. Your score is computed based on the number of correct answers. When you are finished with the test make sure that every question is answered; however, you don't have to answer the question the first time you see it. If you use the coding system you will greatly increase your score.

THE CODING SYSTEM

Over the years COMEX has perfected a systematic approach to taking a multiple choice examination. This is called the coding system. It is designed to:

1. Get you through the examination as quickly as possible.
2. Have you quickly answer those questions that are easy for you.
3. Prevent time wasted on those questions that are too difficult.
4. Take advantage of all your knowledge of a particular subject. Most people think they can get credit only by knowing an answer is correct. You can also prove your knowledge by knowing an answer is incorrect. The coding system will show you how to accomplish this.
5. Get all the help possible by using the recall factor. Because you are going to read the total examination, it is possible that something in question 50 will trigger a thought that will help you answer question 3 the second time you read it.
6. Have your questions prioritized for the second reading.

HOW THE CODING SYSTEM WORKS

We are now going to make you a better test-taker, by showing all of your knowledge and using your time to the greatest advantage. Managing your time on the exam can be as important as knowing the correct answers. If you spend too much time working on difficult questions which you have no knowledge about, you might not get to some easy questions later that you would have gotten correct. This could cause a significant decrease in you score.

Let us attack some sample questions:

1. George Washington was:

   a. the father of King George Washington
   b. the father of Farah Washington
   c. the father of the Washington Laundry
   d. the father of Washington State
   e. the father of our country

As you read the questions you will eliminate all **wrong** answers:

    a. father of King George WashingtonNO!
    b. father of Farah WashingtonNO!
    c. father of the Washington Laundry   NO!
    d. father of Washington State NO!
    e. the father of our country   YES. LEAVE IT ALONE.

The question now looks like this:

1.   George Washington was:

    a. ~~the father of King George Washington~~
    b. ~~the father of Farah Washington~~
    c. ~~the father of the Washington Laundry~~
    d. ~~the father of Washington State~~
    e. the father of our country

Click on the button next to the correct answer and click Next.

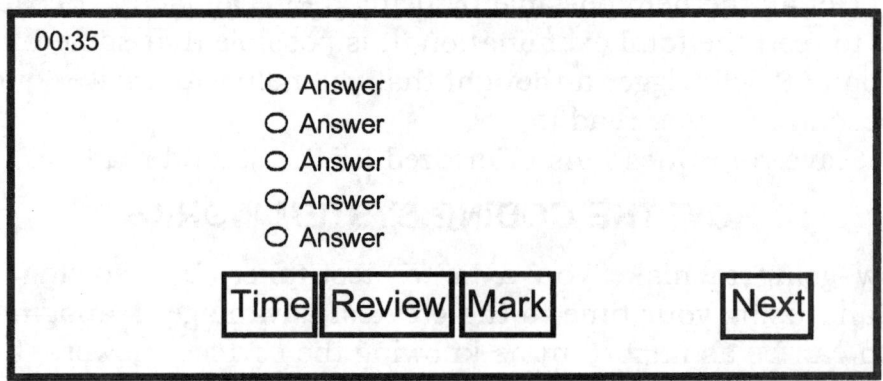

These are the buttons you must know how to use!

You are now finished with this question. Later when you get to the review process this question will be sorted as answered. This will be your signal to not spend any more time with this question. Any time spent will be wasted.

2.   Abraham Lincoln was responsible for:

    a. freeing the 495 freeway
    b. freeing the slaves
    c. freeing the Lincoln Memorial
    d. freeing the south for industrialization
    e. freeing the Potomac River

Go through the answers.

     a. freeing the 495 freeway   No!
     b. freeing the slaves   Maybe. Always read full question.
     c. freeing the Lincoln Memorial   No!
     d. freeing the south for industrialization   Maybe.
     e. freeing the Potomac River   No!

The question now looks like this:

2.   Abraham Lincoln was responsible for:

     a. ~~freeing the 495 freeway~~
     b. freeing the slaves
     c. ~~freeing the Lincoln Memorial~~
     d. freeing the south for industrialization
     e. ~~freeing the Potomac River~~

Should you guess? You have very good odds of getting this question correct. Pick the choice that you feel is the best answer. Often your first guess will be the best. Before clicking the Next button, click on the Mark box. This will tell you later that you were able to eliminate 3 answers before guessing. Now click on Next to go on to the next question.

3.   Franklin Roosevelt's greatest accomplishment was:

     a. building the Panama Canal
     b. solving the Great Depression
     c. putting America to work
     d. organizing the CCC Corps
     e. instituting the income tax

Go through the answers:

a. building the Panama Canal	No! That was a different Roosevelt.
b. solving the Great Depression	Maybe. Go on to the next answer.
c. putting America to work	Maybe. On to the next answer.
d. organizing the CCC Corps	Maybe. On to the next answer.
e. instituting the income tax	Maybe. Leave it alone!

The question now looks like this:

3. Franklin Roosevelt's greatest accomplishment was:

   a. ~~building the Panama Canal~~
   b. solving the Great Depression
   c. putting America to work
   d. organizing the CCC Corps
   e. instituting the income tax

Should you answer this question now? Not yet. There might be a question later that contains information that would help you eliminate more of the answers. When you can only eliminate one answer, or none at all, your best course of action is to simply click on Next. This will bring up the next question.

Now look at another question:

4. Casper P. Phudd III was noted for:

   a. rowing a boat
   b. sailing a boat
   c. building a boat
   d. designing a boat
   e. navigating a boat

Even if you have no idea of who Casper P. Phudd III is, read the answers:

   a. rowing a boat   I do not know.
   b. sailing a boat   I do not know.
   c. building a boat I do not know.
   d. designing a boat   I do not know.
   e. navigating a boat   I do not know.

Since you cannot eliminate any of the answers, simply go on to the next question.

Try another question:

5. Clarence Q. Jerkwater III

   a. sailed the Atlantic Ocean
   b. drained the Atlantic Ocean
   c. flew over the Atlantic Ocean
   d. colored the Atlantic Ocean orange
   e. swam in the Atlantic Ocean

Even though you know nothing of Clarence Q. Jerkwater III, you read the answers.

    a. sailed the Atlantic Ocean   Possible.
    b. drained the Atlantic Ocean No way!
    c. flew over the Atlantic Ocean   Maybe.
    d. colored the Atlantic Ocean orange   No way!
    e. swam in the Atlantic Ocean   Maybe.

The question now looks like this:

5.   Clarence Q. Jerkwater III

    a. sailed the Atlantic Ocean
    b. ~~drained the Atlantic Ocean~~
    c. flew over the Atlantic Ocean
    d. ~~colored the Atlantic Ocean orange~~
    e. swam in the Atlantic Ocean

Do you take a guess? Not on the first reading of the answers. Let us wait to see if the recall factor will help. Do not click on an answer, but do click on Mark. Then click on Next to get the next question.

Continue in this manner until you finish all the questions in the section. By working in this manner you have organized the questions to maximize your efficiency. When you finish with the last question click on Review. This brings up the listing of all the questions. They will be listed in numerical order. This is not the way you want to view them. You sorted the questions as you went through them. You want to view the questions sorted. Click on Status. Now the questions are sorted for you. Let's review what each type means:

Answered without a check mark.
You knew the correct answer.

Answered with a check mark.
You eliminated three answers.

Not answered with a check mark.
You eliminated two answers.

Not answered without a check mark.
You could not eliminate more than one answer.

The Second Time Through

Now you are ready to start your way through the test the second time. Where do you have the best chance of increasing your score? This question should always be at the top of your mind. "How do I show the maximum amount of information I know?" The best place to start is with the questions that you had some idea about, but not enough to answer. These are the questions where you could eliminate two answers. They are marked with a check mark. Clicking on Review, and then Status will sort the questions for you. All of the questions that are marked but have not been answered are grouped together for you.

Click on the first one in the group. Reread the question and the answers. Did anything in any of the other questions give you information to allow you to eliminate any answers? If the answer is yes that is great! The coding system has worked. If you eliminated one more answer make your guess between the remaining two. Leave the Mark box checked and click on Review to go back to the question list to choose your next question. What if you now know the correct answer? Mark it, and **remove** the check from the Mark box. This question will now be listed as answered. You will not spend any more time on this question. Click on Review to go back to your list of questions.

What should you do if you were unable to eliminate any more answers. Now you still need to guess. While your odds are not as good as if you had eliminated three answers, you will have a better chance than if you had eliminated no answers. Any time you eliminate answers before guessing means you are making an educated guess. Every educated guess you make has a higher chance of being correct than a random guess. More educated guesses means a higher score. Leave the Mark box checked. This indicates that you were not sure of your answer.

Continue with this process until you finish all the questions in the group with a check mark that were not answered. Which questions should you work on next? It is now time to work on the questions you had the least knowledge about. These are the questions without a check mark that are not answered. Use the same process that you used for the previous set of questions. Can you now figure out the correct answer? If so mark it and check the box. If not eliminate as many answers as you can and then choose your best answer. If you guess make sure you check the mark box. Every time you reread a question there is a chance that it will trigger something in your memory that will help you with this question, or with one of the others.

Be very careful to keep track of time. If it is not diplayed at the top of the screen, make sure you click on the box so that it will be displayed. Do not think of the clock as your enemy. It is your friend. It keeps you on your task and keeps you moving efficiently through the test.

When you only have 5 minutes left, make sure that you have every question answered. Remember a blank space counts the same as a wrong answer. If you go through and make an educated guess at all the questions, you will get a better score than if the questions were left blank. Even if you randomly guess you should end up with one correct answer out of every five. Every correct answer will increase your score. While you are guessing, make sure you check the mark box, so that you know you guessed on that question. This allows you to review that question later if time permits.

You are now finally at the point where you only have two types of questions left, those where you knew the correct answer and those where you guessed at the answer. All of the questions are now answered. Does this mean it is time to stop? Not if you want to get your highest score. All of the questions on which you took educated guess have a check mark. Keep working on those problems. Do not waste time looking at any questions that do not have a check. You knew the correct answer and are done with them.

By using the coding system you will move quickly through the test and make sure that you see every question. It also allows you to concentrate your efforts on your strongest areas.

Practice the system while you do your exercises and tests. You can use a similar system with a piece of scratch paper. Put an "A" next to questions as you answer them. Put a check mark next to a question to refer back to it. Then use the system to go back through the test. The system is easy to master and will be an invaluable tool in your test-taking arsenal.

You have now completed the portion of this book which is designed to improve your test-taking ability. When you do the practice exercises and take the sample test, use these techniques you have just learned.

You can use the coding system on any multiple choice exam. This will not only increase your score on that test, but it will also make you more comfortable with using the system. It has been demonstrated many times that the more comfortable you are when you are taking a test the higher your score will be.

SOME BASICS FOR THE TEST DAY

1. Get to the examination location early. If you are taking the examination at a new location - check out how to get there **before** the day of the examination.

2. Choose a seat carefully.
   a. In a large room, choose a quiet corner. If possible, sit facing a wall.
   b. If you go with a friend, do not sit together.

3. Stay with your usual routine. If you normally skip breakfast, do so on the test day as well.

4. If you do not understand the proctor's directions, ask questions.

5. Do not quit. Keep going over questions you were not able to answer the first time. You may work anywhere in each section. Beat the examination, do not let it beat you!

6. If you cannot answer a question, code it and go on to the next. Do not spend a lot of time on one question unless you have already finished the rest of that section. Go through each section and do the easiest questions first, then go back to the difficult ones.

7. **Be sure** you understand the directions for **each** type of test **BEFORE you take the examination**. Not understanding the directions can cause you to lose valuable time when you are taking the actual test.

8. Remember to use the coding system.

9. If you are unfamiliar with how to use a mouse, try to get some practice. Most libraries have computers where you can practice. If you have to learn how to use the mouse at the test site you are putting yourself at a severe disadvantage.

Introduction To Review For The CLEP General Examination In English Composition

This study guide is designed to help you prepare for the CLEP General Examination in English Composition.

The best way to use this review is to go through the material in the order presented, studying the information, completing the exercises, and checking your answers. At the end of the review section there is a short practice examination with explanatory answers. In addition, there is a full-length English examination at the end of the book.

The test itself is designed to measure competency in expository writing skills following the conventions of standard written English. Exposition is designed to set forth ideas and facts. Its essential quality is clarity; its appeal is to the intellect of the reader. It encompasses most of the writing a college student is required to do: reports, essays, summaries, reviews, analyses. It does not include fiction or poetry.

The following graph gives you a quick overview of the content you can expect to find on the exam.

Skill Type	Question Type	Test With Essay Percentage	Test Without Essay Percentage
Sentence Level Skills	Identifying Sentence Errors Improving Sentences Restructuring Sentences	30%	55%
Skills in Context	Revising Work in Progress Analyzing Writing	20%	45%
Writing an Essay		50%	0%

The official description of the CLEP English Composition test can be found at www.collegeboard.com.

The first section will examine what is meant by "standard written English."

1

Levels Of Usage

Language is a lot like clothing. If it is inappropriate in a given situation, it calls attention to itself and detracts from the speaker's message. Using slang in a formal essay would be the same as wearing blue jeans to a formal dinner dance.

The level of usage on which you will be expected to operate in the CLEP English examination, and in any formal academic writing, is standard written English.

This level of usage is the language of our institutions: school, business, and government. It is characterized by:

1. Strict attention to the formal rules of grammar and usage
2. Elimination of contractions and shortened forms of words
3. Adherence to the rules of complete sentence structure
4. Elimination of slang and colloquialisms

Informal standard English is conversational language, sometimes labeled "colloquial" in dictionaries. The sentences below illustrate the difference between informal and formal English.

INFORMAL: Most everyone went out of their way to find the kid's bike.

FORMAL: Everyone went out of his way to find the child's bicycle.

The exercise on the next page will test your ability to choose the formal way of saying something.

PRACTICE ON LEVELS OF USAGE

DIRECTIONS: Of the choices given in each of the following sentences, which would be the appropriate one in formal written English? Underline the correct answer.

1. My sister looks exactly (like, as) my mother.

2. Someone mentioned (his, their) favorite magazine to Fred.

3. This person was (real, very) excited about it.

4. That is (she, her) over there.

5. She never told me (who, whom) she was going to ask to the dance.

6. You should not act as if I (was, were) your enemy.

7. When it is very hot, my dog (lays, lies) in the shade.

8. (Like, As) I said before, I admire him greatly.

9. He did (good, well) on the exam.

10. My friend runs much faster than (I, me).

ANSWERS:

1. like   <u>Like</u> is a preposition which is needed here to link the noun <u>mother</u> to the sentence.

2. his   <u>Someone</u> is considered singular and is referred to by the singular masculine pronoun.

3. very   <u>Real</u> is an adjective meaning genuine. The adverb <u>very</u> is needed to modify the participle <u>excited</u>.

4. she   <u>Be</u> verbs are followed by nominative case pronouns.

5. whom   The objective pronoun <u>whom</u> is needed to act as the object of the verb <u>ask</u>.

6. were   In this "if construction" (contrary to fact) the subjunctive <u>were</u> is needed.

7. lies   The verb <u>lie</u>, <u>lying</u>, <u>lay</u>, <u>lain</u> means <u>to rest</u> or <u>recline</u>.

8. As   The subordinate conjunction <u>as</u> is needed to introduce the clause.

9. well   The adverb <u>well</u> is needed to modify the verb <u>did</u>.

10. I   <u>I</u> is the subject of the incomplete construction "faster than I can run."

How did you do? It is not important that you know the grammar involved in the explanations; it is there for the benefit of those who are curious. If you had a great deal of trouble with this exercise, or if you do not feel confident about grammar in general, you might want to review it on your own. Space will not permit an extensive formal grammar review in this text. However, grammatical concepts are included when they relate to the writing skills being taught in a particular section, or when they are important for your ability to answer a specific type of test question. There is also a review of grammar rules and terminology at the end of the book.

The glossary on the next page provides brief definitions of terms related to levels of usage and writing.

A Glossary For Grammar And Usage Study

ambiguity   a possible double meaning that may confuse a listener or reader

colloquial   used in some dictionaries to label words appropriate only in informal speech

consistency   the result of staying within one pattern and avoiding confusing shifts in tense or grammatical perspective

convention   the customary way of doing things; what a reader or listener expects or is accustomed to

economy   the sparing use of words, avoiding unnecessary wordiness or duplication

formal   the kind of English appropriate in serious discussion and writing

grammar   the study of the forms of words and their arrangement in a language

informal   the kind of standard English we use in casual conversations and personal letters

non-standard   the everyday language of those with little formal education; inappropriate in school, business, or writing

redundancy   unintentional repetition, needless duplication

slang   extremely informal language; often used in a disrespectful manner

standard   the language of our institutions - of school, church, business, and government

Diction

Written language must be more precise than spoken language. It must be capable of standing without additional explanation and without voice inflection and facial expression to clarify meaning. For this reason, you must be far more careful in choosing words when you are writing than when you are speaking.

Diction means word choice. Since words are the tool of a writer, it is important for a person who hopes to write to develop a good vocabulary. In addition, those who read a great deal have a tendency to be better writers than those who do not. The reason is obvious. Reading makes one more familiar with patterns in language, enriches the vocabulary, and provides new ideas.

This section will examine some of the problems involved in diction.

1. CONNOTATION AND DENOTATION

Looking up a word in the dictionary is only the beginning of understanding it. Every word has an objective definition referred to as its **denotation**. However, just as important are the emotional associations we have with a word. These associations are called the **connotation** of a word. For example: fat, obese, and portly have denotations that are almost identical. However, each word would be used in a different situation and would produce a different effect. An obese person is a very fat person. A portly person is stout in a dignified manner. Of the three, you would probably be least insulted by being called "portly."

Many writers rely heavily on the thesaurus, a dictionary of synonyms. This is a valuable tool, and it can be very helpful in allowing you to avoid monotonous repetition. However, caution is necessary. Remember that no two words mean exactly the same thing. Be aware of the connotations of the words you are using.

The following exercise will illustrate this point.

PRACTICE WITH CONNOTATION AND DENOTATION

DIRECTIONS: This exercise tests your ability to choose the word with the right connotations. For each sentence, choose the word that best fits the context.

1. Our _____ boss greeted us with a smile and an occasional word of praise.

    (A) surly
    (B) taciturn
    (C) laconic

2. Corporations are always looking for _____ sales representatives.

    (A) aggressive
    (B) heroic
    (C) courageous

3. The rules were oppressive because they were _____ applied.

    (A) strictly
    (B) rigidly
    (C) intelligently

4. People were shocked when the President chose a _____ liar as his Press Secretary.

    (A) famous
    (B) heroic
    (C) notorious

5. Our biggest complaint about the boss is the way he _____ us constantly about petty things.

    (A) nags
    (B) reproaches
    (C) reprimands

6. The men who refused to obey the captain's orders were tried for
   _____.

   (A) revolution
   (B) insurrection
   (C) mutiny

7. The teacher did not _____ the students' behavior at the assembly.

   (A) approve of
   (B) ratify
   (C) acclaim

8. Some people like to _____ over prices at antique markets.

   (A) discuss
   (B) haggle
   (C) debate

9. The review praised the author for his _____ gift of expression.

   (A) unique
   (B) eccentric
   (C) peculiar

10. The _____ of a tyrant is sometimes regarded as a blow for liberty
    rather than as a crime.

    (A) murder
    (B) manslaughter
    (C) assassination

ANSWERS:

1. (B) taciturn — Someone is taciturn if he habitually prefers to keep silent.

2. (A) aggressive — An aggressive sales representative would be bold and active.

3. (B) rigidly — If rules are rigidly applied, they are applied without thought or adjustment to circumstances.

4. (C) notorious — Notorious people are well-known for negative things.

5. (A) nags — Nagging is finding fault repeatedly, usually for insignificant things.

6. (C) mutiny — A mutiny is the rebellion of a ship's crew against their captain.

7. (A) approve of — The teacher did not have a favorable opinion of the behavior.

8. (B) haggle — To haggle means to argue about price.

9. (A) unique — Something unique is one-of-a-kind, in a positive sense.

10. (C) assassination — The word assassination is used to describe the politically motivated killing of a person in power.

If you had a problem with any of these questions, it would be beneficial to look up the words in a dictionary for exact definition. Remember that, in addition, the habitual emotional and contextual associations of the words must be considered. For example: as an author (question 9), would you rather have your style considered unique, eccentric or peculiar? Of the three, unique is the most favorable word. In question 7, all three words denote approval, but ratify and acclaim are too formal for this context.

2. TROUBLESOME WORD PAIRS

There are pairs of words in English that tend to give writers trouble. Many of these words are homonyms (words that are pronounced the same but are spelled differently, such as <u>here</u> and <u>hear</u>). Others present grammatical problems, such as <u>leave</u> and <u>let</u>. Most of these are very frequently used parts of our daily vocabulary.

The following list includes explanations of some of these troublesome words. You should master the pairs given. Actively study and think of your own personal way to differentiate between the words, and you will never forget them.

This is by no means an exhaustive list of such troublesome pairs. Be alert for others in various exercises and in your daily reading and writing. Add those new words to this list.

SOME TROUBLESOME WORD PAIRS

ACCEPT/EXCEPT	To **accept** (verb) is to receive or agree to. He **accepted** my gift. To **except** (verb) is to leave out. In giving assignments, the teacher **excepted** those who were absent the day before. **Except** (preposition) also means **but**. Everyone is invited **except** you.
AFFECT/EFFECT	To **affect** (verb) is to influence. His father's death **affected** him deeply. To **effect** (verb) is to bring about. The new president **effected** many changes in the company. **Effect** (noun) is a result. The **effect** of the drug on the disease is unknown.

ALL READY/ALREADY	**All ready** (pronoun + adjective) means everyone is ready.
	When she arrived, we were **all ready** to go.
	Already (adverb) means previously. Mark has **already** gone to school.
ALL RIGHT/ALRIGHT	**All right** means entirely correct, perfectly well.
	It is **all right** (not alright) for you to leave now.
	Alright - this word is not recorded in any standard dictionary and is to be avoided.
BESIDE/BESIDES	**Beside** means next to, or close to.
	He stood **beside** her.
	Besides means in addition to.
	Two players, **besides** the captain, received letters in football.
BRING/TAKE	**Bring** means carry toward the speaker. Please **bring** me the book.
	Take means carry away from the speaker. Please **take** my coat upstairs.

CAPITAL/CAPITOL	**Capital** (noun) means a city, or money used by business. What is the **capital** of Pennsylvania? Do you have enough **capital** to begin your business venture? **Capital** (adjective) also means punishable by death or of major importance. Killing a police officer is a **capital** offense in some states. **Capitol** is a building; a statehouse. What street is the **Capitol** on?
COMPLEMENT/ COMPLIMENT	To **complement** means to complete. The scarf was a perfect **complement** to her wardrobe. To **compliment** means to praise. She accepted our **compliment** on her dress gracefully.
CONTEMPTIBLE/ CONTEMPTUOUS	**Contemptible** means deserving of scorn; **contemptuous** means feeling scorn. The athlete who was **contemptuous** toward his opponent was **contemptible**.
DESERT/DESSERT	**Desert** (noun) - arid region. Camels are supposed to be good at crossing the **desert**. **Desert** (verb) - to leave You should not **desert** your friends when they need you. **Dessert** (noun) - the final course of a meal. Marge always serves cheese cake for **dessert**.

EVERY DAY/EVERYDAY	**Every day** is used as an adverb. He comes to look at the same statue in the museum **every day**. **Everyday** is used as an adjective. His trip to the museum is an **everyday** occurrence.
FARTHER/FURTHER	Generally interchangeable, though many persons prefer **farther** in expressions of physical distance and **further** in expressions of time, quantity, and degree. My car went **farther** than his. The second speaker went **further** into the issues than the first.
FEWER/LESS	**Fewer** is used to refer to a number of things. **Less** is used to refer to a quantity of one thing. Use **fewer** if the word modified is plural; use **less** if the word modified is singular. There are **fewer** apples in this basket. There is **less** fruit in this basket.
IMPLY/INFER	**Imply** means to give hints. His tone of voice **implied** that he was in favor of the idea. **Infer** means to receive hints. We **inferred** from his comments that he was in agreement with the proposition.
IT'S/ITS	**It's** means it is. **It's** Tuesday. **Its** means belonging to it. The dog lost its bone.

LAY/LIE	To **lay** is to put or place. Its principal parts are **lay**, **laid**, (has) **laid**, **laying**. He **laid** the book on the table. To **lie** means to rest or recline. Principal parts are **lie**, **lay**, (has) **lain**, **lying**. The book **lay** there all day.
LEAVE/LET	**Leave** means to go away. When will the bus **leave**? **Let** means to allow. **Let** us take a walk to the beach.
LEAD/LED	**Lead** (noun) is a metal. The boots are as heavy as **lead**. **Lead** is the present form of the verb meaning to go first. The past tense of this verb is **led**. Tomorrow I will **lead** the way; yesterday John **led** the way.
LOOSE/LOSE	**Loose** (rhymes with moose) means free, not closely bound. The string on the package is too **loose**. **Lose** is to suffer a loss. Do not **lose** your lunch money.
LIKE/AS	Use **like** as a preposition; use **as**, **as if**, or **as though** as a conjunction. Preposition: She acted **like** a novice. Conjunction: She acted **as if** (**as though**) she had never been in a movie before.

OF/HAVE	**Of** (preposition) Give me a drink **of** water. **Have** (a verb) I would **have** liked it. AREA OF CONFUSION: We could **have** (NOT <u>OF</u>) done it if we had tried. We need the verb, HAVE here. Do not be confused by the tendency to slur this in speech to the contraction could've.
PRINCIPLE/PRINCIPAL	**Principle** (noun) means underlying rule. The teacher explained some **principles** of grammar. **Principal** (noun) - head of a school Our school has a new **principal**. **Principal** (adjective) also means main. Cotton is the **principal** crop of that area.
REAL/REALLY	**Real** is an adjective. He is a **real** friend. **Really** is an adverb. I am **really** (not real) glad to see you.
RISE/RAISE	The verb **rise** means to go up. Its principal parts are **rise, rose, risen, rising**. The sun **rises** each morning. The verb **raise** means to force something to move upward. Its principal parts are **raise, raised, raising**. **Raise** your hand before speaking

THAN/THEN	**Than** is a conjunction used in comparisons.
	Try to find someone shorter **than** Marty.
	Then is an adverb meaning at that time.
	Then he ran up the stairs.
THEIR/THERE/THEY'RE	**Their** (belonging to them) shows ownership.
	They brought **their** pencils.
	There is an adverb meaning in that place.
	Have you ever been **there**?
	They're means they are.
	They're late for class again.
TO/TWO/TOO	**To** is a preposition. Give it **to** me.
	Two is a number I lost **two** dollars.
	Too means excessively and is required in sentences such as, "I am **too** tired to work."
	Too means also. May I go, **too**?
WHO'S/WHOSE	**Who's**, meaning who is.
	Who's at the door? (who is)
	Whose, meaning belonging to whom. **Whose** book is that?

YOUR/YOU'RE	**Your** means belonging to you.
	I have **your** book.
	You're (contraction) meaning you are.
	Do you know where **you're** going? (you are)

Practice with Troublesome Pairs

DIRECTIONS: Choose the correct word to fit the context of each sentence.

1.   Gary has (all ready, already) handed in his paper.

2.   (All right, Alright), I'll answer the phone this time.

3.   This poison has a deadly (affect, effect).

4.   Sacramento is the (capital, capitol) of California.

5.   The engineer designed an irrigation project for the (desert, dessert).

6.   I passed your sincere (compliment, complement) along to Randy.

7.   The class is very proud of (its, it's) progress.

8.   Facing certain defeat, the troops did not (lose, loose) courage.

9.   Mr. Smith is the (principal, principle) of our school.

10.   Tell Spot to (lie, lay) down in front of the fireplace.

11.   What did you do (than, then)?

12.   (They're, Their, There) are the books you lost.

13.   I am (too, to, two) tired to go to the party.

14.   We (implied, inferred) from the book that the author had done a great deal of research on Egyptian art.

15.   Please (take, bring) this book to the library.

ANSWERS:

1. already
2. All right
3. effect
4. capital
5. desert
6. compliment
7. its
8. lose
9. principal
10. lie
11. then
12. There
13. too
14. inferred
15. take

If you had any problems with these questions, review the definitions of the words involved on the preceding pages.

3. IDIOMS

An idiom is a phrase in which the meaning of the whole expression is different from the total meanings of the words of which it is composed. Although every language has its own idiomatic expressions, English seems to have an especially large number.

Idioms are especially difficult for people who learn English as a second or third language. A native speaker knows very well what someone means by the expression, "hit the nail on the head." A newcomer to our language might rightly inquire, "What nail?" or "Whose head?"

Many English idioms are verb phrases (verb + preposition), such as put out, put up, put down. In formal writing you should use the correct idiomatic expression.

Look at the following list of prepositional idioms. Check off and study the ones that you think you would have a tendency to misuse.

Not Idiomatic	Idiomatic
accused with	accused of
agree with (a plan or idea)	agree to (a plan or idea)
adequate for	adequate to
angry at (a person)	angry with (a person)
cannot help but	cannot help
comply to	comply with
different than	different from
doubt if	doubt that, doubt whether
frightened of	frightened by or at
identical to	identical with
in accordance to	in accordance with
in search for	in search of
intend on doing	intend to do
in the year of 1978	in the year 1978
off of	off
plan on	plan to
privilege to	privilege of
superior than	superior to
try and see	try to see
type of a	type of

4. CLICHÉS

Clichés are expressions which have become stale through too frequent use. Once striking, they have lost their suggestive value. There is nothing inherently wrong with such expressions as: "bull in a china shop", "blanket of snow", "true blue", or "tired but happy", but they have been used so much that they may bore your reader and weaken the effect of your writing. Trite expressions come to mind so readily that they will probably turn up in your writing unless you make a special effort to avoid them. Remember, the simple, straightforward statement of an idea is better than a worn-out expression.

It is not necessary to study a list of clichés. You will recognize them as soon as you encounter them if you are alert.

Here is a brief list of trite expressions and an example of a better, more direct way of expressing the same idea.

Cliché	Straightforward
bid a fond farewell	say good-bye
green with envy	extremely envious
beat a hasty retreat	left quickly
burn the midnight oil	work very late
fell into the arms of Morpheus	went to sleep
a sea of faces	a crowd
true blue	Loyal

The point is that the most effective way to say something is not with a cliché. As much as possible, try to use straightforward language in expository writing.

DIRECTIONS: The following passage contains a number of trite expressions or clichés. Underline as many as you can find.

A good time was had by all at the party. When someone spilled a drink on the new carpet, the host commented that accidents will happen. However, to add insult to injury, another guest dropped a plate of spaghetti in the same spot. He beat a hasty retreat to the kitchen for a cloth to clean up the mess. It was clear as crystal that the professional rug cleaners would get a call the next day, for cleaning this mess without benefit of complicated machinery was easier said than done. To make a long story short, a sadder but wiser host vowed not to serve spaghetti at his next party.

ANSWERS:

A good time was had by all
accidents will happen
to add insult to injury
beat a hasty retreat
clear as crystal
easier said than done
To make a long story short
sadder but wiser

5. MIXED FIGURES OF SPEECH

A figure of speech is an expression in which words are used regardless of their true meaning in order to create a more vivid impression or produce a special effect. Many of our common clichés fall into the category of figures of speech: "muscles of steel", "cool as a cucumber", "sly as a fox".

A person who is in the habit of observing and comparing will be able to write good figures of speech. It is possible to use them in expository writing without being flowery, pretentious, or trite. You should be aware, however, of one error which is easily made in the use of figures of speech. This is the fault of mixing two different comparisons; in other words, of failing to stay with one comparison once you have made it. For example:

MIXED: His joke sank like a soggy cake, and he refused a second shot at the target of making his audience laugh.

(This example starts out with <u>sinking</u> and moves to <u>shooting</u>.)

BETTER: His joke <u>sank</u> like a soggy cake, and he refused to try to keep a second one <u>afloat</u> in order to make his audience laugh.

6. REDUNDANCY

Some writers confuse the amount of writing with the quality of writing. They mistakenly believe that a 500-word essay is always better than a 250-word essay. On the contrary, most good writing is effective because it is not cluttered with unnecessary words. A cardinal principle of writing is to avoid wordiness by eliminating superfluous words and unnecessary repetition of ideas.

Sometimes redundancy results from the lack of knowledge of the meaning of a word. For example: "descend down", "repeat again", "visible to the eye", "rise up", "audible to the ear", "return back". In all cases, only the first word of the expression is necessary because the second part means the same thing.

PRACTICE ON FIGURES OF SPEECH AND REDUNDANCY

DIRECTIONS: Choose the best completion for each sentence. Be concerned with consistently maintaining figures of speech and avoiding redundancy.

1. Business enterprise disappeared in the wintry blasts of the recession, and capital seemed to ...

   (A) decrease to nothing.
   (B) hide from sight.
   (C) be buried under the ice.
   (D) melt.

2. The diagnosis was correct, but the remedy offered would not...

   (A) smother the flame.
   (B) cure the disease.
   (C) solve the problem.
   (D) light the fire.

3. The first story in the book is...

    (A) a masterpiece in itself.
    (B) a masterpiece in itself and quite a story.
    (C) a masterpiece.
    (D) a well-written masterpiece of writing.

4. We walked out before...

    (A) the final end of the movie.
    (B) the grand finale ending of the movie.
    (C) the final conclusion of the movie.
    (D) the end of the movie.

5. In this green pasture of learning, my mind has...

    (A) climbed to the top of the hill.
    (B) fed on the classics.
    (C) been parched.
    (D) melted from sight.

ANSWERS:

1. (C)   be buried under the ice ... The reference to <u>ice</u> maintains the comparison of economic conditions to <u>a winter storm</u>.

2. (B)   cure the disease ... <u>Disease</u> continues the reference to a <u>remedy</u>.

3. (C)   a masterpiece ... All other answers contain unnecessary words.

4. (D)   the end of the movie ... All other answers contain unnecessary words.

5. (B)   fed on the classics ... <u>Feeding</u> continues the reference to a green pasture.

Ambiguity: Pronoun Reference

Ambiguity results when two or more meanings are possible. It is a vagueness that detracts from good expository writing.

One of the chief causes of ambiguity is careless use of pronouns. Let's examine this area in more detail. There are four common ways to avoid ambiguity that results from improper pronoun usage.

#1 GIVE PRONOUNS CLEAR ANTECEDENTS

A pronoun is a word (such as he, she, it, who, etc.) that takes the place of a noun. It is important to note that in writing, the noun that the pronoun refers to must be clearly stated. This noun is called the **antecedent** of the pronoun.

EXAMPLE: Allison told Sue that she was too tired to go.

It is not clear whether the pronoun she points to Allison or Sue. In order to clarify this particular problem, the sentence could be rewritten in two ways.

REVISION: Allison told Sue that Allison was too tired to go.

or

Allison said, "Sue, I am too tired to go."

Remember, make sure that it is absolutely clear to your reader which noun any pronoun refers to. In speaking, you may point or nod your head, but writing must be clear as it stands.

#2 AVOID GENERAL REFERENCE

General reference occurs when a pronoun refers confusingly to a general idea which is vague to the reader. The pronouns this, that, it, and which are often used in this way.

EXAMPLE: The boys were playing in the kitchen which I disapproved of.

In this sentence, the pronoun which refers to the general idea playing in the kitchen. In addition, the pronoun is placed so that it appears to refer to kitchen. The sentence can be corrected by this revision.

REVISION: I disapproved of the boys' playing in the kitchen.

#3 AVOID WEAK REFERENCE

Weak reference occurs when the antecedent of the pronoun is not expressed but exists only in the writer's mind.

EXAMPLE: We spent the day fishing but didn't catch a single <u>one</u>.

In this sentence there is no antecedent for the pronoun <u>one</u>. The writer meant the pronoun to stand for the noun <u>fish</u>.

REVISION: We spent the day fishing but didn't catch a single fish.

#4 AVOID THE INDEFINITE USE OF THE PRONOUNS <u>THEY</u>, <u>YOU</u> AND <u>IT</u>

The indefinite use of these pronouns occurs frequently in conversation. However, it is not acceptable in formal writing.

EXAMPLE: On planes <u>they</u> sometimes serve enjoyable meals.

There is no antecedent for the pronoun <u>they</u>.

REVISION: Enjoyable meals are sometimes served on planes.

PRACTICE AVOIDING AMBIGUOUS USE OF PRONOUNS

DIRECTIONS: The following sentences contain ambiguous pronouns. Revise each sentence so that the reference is clear. Remember that there may be several correct revisions possible.

1. The cab driver told one of the passengers that he didn't know where he was going.

2. Don is very good at telling jokes, which makes him fun to be with.

3. When we finally got to the ice cream stand, the waitress told us she didn't have any.

4. In Washington they are skeptical about the possibility of a tax cut.

5. In the paper it says that the stock market is rising.

ANSWERS:

1. <u>He</u> could refer to either the cab driver or the passenger.

    The cab driver said to the passenger, "You don't know where you're going."

    The cab driver said to the passenger, "I don't know where I'm going."

2. <u>Which</u> refers to the whole phrase <u>good at telling jokes</u>.

    Don's ability to tell jokes makes him fun to be with.

3. There is no antecedent for <u>any</u>.

    When we finally got to the ice cream stand, the waitress told us she didn't have any ice cream.

4. <u>They</u> has no antecedent.

    In Washington, legislators are skeptical about a tax cut.

5. <u>It</u> has no antecedent.

    The paper says the stock market is rising.

There are, of course, other possible correct revisions. Just be sure your revision contains no ambiguity.

Ambiguity: Modifiers And Comparisons

A second common cause of ambiguity is the misplacement of modifiers. A modifier is a descriptive word or phrase. The rule is simple: always place a modifier as close as possible to the word it describes.

Here are some examples of problems with modifiers and comparisons.

#1 MISPLACED MODIFIER

EXAMPLE: In this book are facts about crime which the librarian recommended highly.

It sounds as though the librarian is recommending crime.

REVISION: In this book, which the librarian recommended highly, are facts about crime.

#2 DANGLING MODIFIER

EXAMPLE: Climbing the mountain, the town came into view.

Climbing the mountain has nothing to modify. It appears that the town is doing the climbing.

REVISION: While I was climbing the mountain, the town came into view.

#3 TWO-WAY MODIFIERS

EXAMPLE: Tell Hal when he comes home I want to see him.

Do you want to see Hal when he comes home, or do you want him told when he comes home? Both meanings are possible.

REVISION: When Hal comes home, tell him I want to see him.

Ambiguity: Incomplete Comparisons

A third cause of ambiguity is incomplete comparison.

EXAMPLE: Jim is taller than any man I know.

The implication is that Jim is not a man.

REVISION: Jim is taller than any other man I know.

PRACTICE WITH AMBIGUOUS MODIFIERS AND COMPARISONS

DIRECTIONS: The sentences in this exercise contain misplaced, dangling, or two-way modifiers and incomplete comparisons. Revise each sentence so that its meaning will be clear. Remember that there is more than one possible correct revision.

1. While lighting a cigarette, the car swerved dangerously.

2. Did you know when you were here I was ill?

3. This dealer sells cars to customers of all makes.

4. Shakespeare is greater than any writer.

5. Twenty people were reported as injured by doctors at the scene.

ANSWERS:

	TYPE OF ERROR	REVISION
1.	Dangling modifier	While the driver was lighting a cigarette, the car swerved dangerously.
2.	Two-way modifier	When you were here, did you know that I was ill? *OR* Did you know that I was ill when you were here?
3.	Misplaced modifier	This dealer sells cars of all makes to customers.
4.	Incomplete comparison	Shakespeare is greater than any other writer.
5.	Misplaced modifier	Twenty people were reported by doctors at the scene as injured. *OR* Doctors at the scene reported that twenty people were injured.

Sentence Structure

1. DEFINITION

The sentence is the basic grammatical unit important in theme writing. Previous sections of this book have dealt with word choice (diction) and placement of modifiers. The modifiers we have considered were, for the most part, single words, phrases, or clauses. Before we consider sentence structure, it is important to understand these smaller grammatical units. In order to accomplish this, we must first grasp the concept of subject and predicate verb. The **predicate verb** shows action or being. The **subject** is the person or thing doing the action, or being spoken of. To find the subject it is necessary to find the verb and ask "Who?" or "What?"

EXAMPLE: The dog ran to the house.

PREDICATE VERB (THE ACTION): <u>ran</u>

SUBJECT (WHO OR WHAT RAN?) : <u>dog</u>

A **phrase** is a group of words, <u>not</u> containing both a subject and a predicate verb, which act together as a single part of speech. <u>To the house</u>, <u>have been</u>, <u>walking to school</u>, <u>to be</u> president are examples of phrases.

A **clause** is a group of words containing a subject and a predicate verb which forms a sentence, a part of a sentence, or an independent clause. If the clause expresses a complete thought, we call it a **simple sentence**. If it does not, we call it a **dependent clause**.

EXAMPLE: INDEPENDENT CLAUSE

The <u>boy</u> <u>walked</u> the dog.
　　↑　　↑
subject　verb

EXAMPLE: DEPENDENT CLAUSE

while the <u>boy</u> <u>was walking</u> the dog
　　　↑　　↑
　subject　verb

31

Notice how the dependent clause contains a subject and a verb but does not express a complete thought. (Remember that the verb is the action or being word in a sentence. The subject answers the question <u>who</u>? or <u>what</u>?.)

2. THE FRAGMENT

One sentence error to be avoided is the sentence fragment. A **fragment** is a part of a sentence written as though it were a complete sentence. Remember that a complete sentence must meet three requirements:

> It must have a subject.
> It must have a verb.
> It must express a complete thought.

If a group of words does not meet all three of these requirements, it is considered to be a **fragment**.

EXAMPLES: Waiting for her mother to pick her up after school.

> After the game was over.

> The boy walking the dog.

This error is most frequently made in writing when the fragment is closely related to the preceding sentence.

EXAMPLE: Don wanted us to pick him up. After the game was over.

The first group of words is a sentence; however, the second group is not, although it does make sense in its position. A possible way to correct the error would be by joining the two groups of words.

REVISION: Don wanted us to pick him up after the game was over.

3. COORDINATION

There are several acceptable ways to join dependent and independent clauses to form sentences. If these clauses are not connected properly, both by connectives and punctuation, the result is a **run-on sentence**.

Two independent clauses may be joined to form a compound sentence in the following ways:

English is my favorite subject, but I don't like math.

English is my favorite subject; I don't like math.

English is my favorite subject; however, I don't like math.

It would be incorrect to separate the two complete thoughts only with a comma. The three correct ways are a comma and coordinating conjunction (and, but, or, nor, for, yet); a semicolon; a semicolon and a conjunctive adverb (however, moreover, therefore, etc.). Remember that a semicolon implies a closer relationship between sentences than a period does.

When you write a compound sentence, you are saying that both ideas are equally important, and both should carry equal weight with the reader. You are coordinating ideas.

4. EXCESSIVE COORDINATION

Excessive use of coordination fails to show precise relationships between ideas. It is not usually true that every idea you wish to express should carry equal weight. In addition, a theme or paragraph consisting of nothing but simple or compound sentences tends to be monotonous. Another result of excessive coordination is stringiness.

STRINGY: The dog weighs fifty pounds, and he is very shaggy, but he loves to jump on people's laps and pretend to be a baby.

IMPROVED: Although the dog weighs fifty pounds and is very shaggy, he loves to jump on people's laps and pretend to be a baby.

The key is that you should decide which ideas you wish to emphasize. These ideas belong in main clauses. Lesser ideas belong in dependent clauses.

5. SUBORDINATION

Another type of English sentence is the complex sentence. This type consists of an independent clause and one or more dependent clauses.

EXAMPLE: <u>Although it was raining</u>, <u>everyone enjoyed the picnic.</u>

              ↑   ↑

     dependent clause   independent clause

Notice how the meaning changes when we change the relationship of ideas.

<u>Although everyone enjoyed the picnic</u>, <u>it was raining</u>.

              ↑   ↑

     dependent clause   independent clause

In the first sentence emphasis is on the fact that everyone enjoyed the picnic. The rain is incidental. In the second sentence the important idea is that it was raining.

Coordination and subordination may be combined in a compound-complex sentence which contains two independent clauses and one or more dependent clauses.

6. AVOID OVERLAPPING OF SUBORDINATE CONSTRUCTIONS

Do not string too many dependent clauses together.

EXAMPLE: A car is an intricate machine which provides transportation which many people regard as an essential commodity that is necessary for survival in the suburbs.

IMPROVED: The car, which many regard as essential for survival in the suburbs, is an intricate machine made to provide transportation.

Notice how the revision clears up some ambiguity. In the original, it is not clear whether it is the car or transportation that is necessary for survival in the suburbs. It could be either.

```
┌─────────────────────────────────────────────────────────────┐
│                    POINTS TO REMEMBER:                        │
│                                                               │
│   1.  A complete sentence must have a subject and a verb      │
│       and must express a complete thought.                    │
│                                                               │
│   2.  Two complete thoughts may be joined to form a           │
│       compound sentence.  (Coordination)                      │
│                                                               │
│   3.  Two or more thoughts of unequal importance may be       │
│       joined to form a complex sentence.  (Subordination)     │
│                                                               │
│   4.  You should avoid fragments, run-ons, excessive          │
│       coordination, and excessive overlapping of subordinate  │
│       constructions.                                          │
│                                                               │
└─────────────────────────────────────────────────────────────┘
```

PRACTICE ON SENTENCE STRUCTURE

DIRECTIONS: Identify the sentence fragments and run-on sentences in
the following exercise. Some of the sentences are correct.

1. One day he brought us a big surprise. A large spider.

2. Ken liked shop best of all his classes, he was good at making things
out of wood.

3. Although my friend is not fond of mushrooms, he will eat them on
cheesecake.

4. The dog should be free of loose dirt. When you apply the shampoo.

5. Many people are afraid of snakes, for example, Mike will not stay in
the same room with a boa.

DIRECTIONS: Decide whether each of the following sentences is stringy,
has excessive overlapping subordination, or is a well-
written sentence structure.

6. The weather was cold so we decided to stay inside and we sat by the
fire and we read stories but it was fun.

7. Although the service was very slow, we had an enjoyable lunch because the atmosphere was so lovely in the restaurant which is located next to an antique shop.

8. Since it was Friday night, I didn't feel like working; however, I had an important deadline to meet.

9. September is the favorite month of many mothers who are glad to have their children back in school.

10. I finished reading the mystery last night but I won't reveal the ending because I'd like you to enjoy it too since you are almost finished.

ANSWERS:

1. The second group of words is a fragment.

   Correction: One day he brought us a surprise, a large spider.

2. This is a run-on sentence. A comma cannot separate two independent clauses.

   Correction: (There are many possible ones.) Ken liked shop better than all his other classes because he was good at making things out of wood.

3. This is a correct English (complex) sentence.

4. The second group of words is a fragment.

   Correction: The dog should be free of loose dirt when you apply the shampoo.

5. This is a run-on sentence.

   Correction: Many people are afraid of snakes; for example, Mike will not stay in the same room with a boa.

6. Excessive coordination.

   Correction: Since the weather was cold, we decided to stay inside by the fire and read stories; it was fun.

7. Overlapping subordination.

   Correction: Although the service was very slow, we had an enjoyable lunch in the lovely atmosphere of the restaurant located next to the antique shop.

8. This is a correct English (compound-complex) sentence.

9. This is a correct English (complex) sentence.

10. This is a stringy sentence.

   Correction: I finished reading the mystery last night, but I won't reveal the ending. Since you are almost finished, I'd like you to enjoy it too.

Consistency

Consistency is one of the key ingredients in achieving clarity in writing. This section will discuss ways of maintaining consistency in grammatical structure, tense, and voice.

1. PARALLELISM

Examine these two sentences:

> A man that is great is often misunderstood.

> To be great is to be misunderstood.

Why is the second (a quote from Bacon) so much more effective and memorable than the first? The answer is balance achieved through parallel structure. While the first sentence is grammatically correct, the second has an additional quality that is the hallmark of good writing. It would be analyzed grammatically in this way:

> Infinitive + Adjective + Verb + Infinitive + Adjective

It illustrates the rule that ideas that are parallel in thought should be expressed in parallel grammatical forms.

One of the most important places to use parallelism is in a series.

EXAMPLE: He likes running, walking and to swim.

BETTER: He likes running, walking, and swimming.

Remember, use parallel grammatical forms to express elements parallel in thought. Constructions should be parallel in form if they are connected by coordinating conjunctions (and, but, or, nor) or by correlative conjunctions (either...or, neither...nor, both...and, not only...but also). Words go with similar words, phrases with similar phrases, clauses with similar clauses.

2. TENSE

Tense expresses the time of an action. It is important to maintain consistency in tense to avoid confusion. It is also important to know how each tense should be used. Study the following information.

SIMPLE TENSES

The **present** tense indicates present time; some action or condition is now going on or is in progress.

EXAMPLE: I <u>am walking</u> my dog. I <u>walk</u> my dog.

The **past** tense indicates past time; something happened or is already over or done.

EXAMPLE: I <u>walked</u> my dog yesterday.

The **future** tense indicates future time; something is expected to come or happen.

EXAMPLE: I <u>shall walk</u> my dog tomorrow.

PERFECT TENSES

The **present perfect** tense indicates that the action is complete at the present time.

EXAMPLE: I <u>have walked</u> my dog and am ready for dinner.

The **past perfect** tense indicates a past action that will be completed before some other past action.

EXAMPLE: I <u>had walked</u> my dog before Ruth arrived.

The **future perfect** tense indicates an action that will be completed in the future before some other action in the future.

EXAMPLE: I <u>shall have walked</u> my dog before Ruth will arrive.

NOTE: All the perfect tenses are formed by these two elements: an auxiliary verb and the past participle of the main verb.

In general, the tenses are used as follows:

Present Perfect with Present

Past Perfect with Past

Future Perfect with Future

Avoid a confusing shift in tense:

EXAMPLE: As we <u>sat</u> around the fire, I <u>notice</u> a noise in the woods.

        (past)   (present)

CORRECTION: As we <u>sat</u> around the fire, I <u>noticed</u> a noise in the woods.

         (past)   (past)

Remember to be logical and consistent in your use of tenses in writing.

3. VOICE

A verb is either active or passive in voice.

When the subject of the sentence is doing the action, the verb is <u>active</u>.

EXAMPLE: The dog chased the boy. (The subject, <u>dog</u>, is doing the action.)

When the subject of the sentence is acted upon, the verb is <u>passive</u>.

EXAMPLE: The boy was chased by the dog. (The subject, boy, is being acted upon. He is being chased, not chasing.)

In general the passive voice is considered to be the weaker, less effective form. It is to be used sparingly.

In regard to consistency, the rule is to avoid needless shifts from active to passive.

EXAMPLE: He cooks crab for ten minutes and then it is allowed to cool.

BETTER: He <u>cooks</u> crab for ten minutes and then <u>allows</u> it to cool.

4. PRONOUNS

Avoid careless shifts in the person of the pronouns you are using.

EXAMPLE: <u>A person</u> can travel today if <u>you</u> have the patience to stand in line.

<u>A person</u> is third person singular and should be referred to by the third person pronoun <u>he</u>.

REVISION: <u>A person</u> can travel today if <u>he</u> has the patience to stand in line.

NOTE: When we refer to the <u>person</u> of a pronoun, the speaker (<u>I</u> or <u>we</u>) is first person, the person spoken to (<u>you</u>) is second person, and the person or thing spoken about (<u>he</u>, <u>they</u>, <u>she</u>, <u>it</u>) is third person.

5. DIRECT AND INDIRECT DISCOURSE

Direct discourse is the quoting of a person's exact words. Indirect discourse is the paraphrasing of his words. It is confusing to shift from one to the other in the same construction.

EXAMPLE: The teacher says that the book is poorly written and asks why would anyone buy it.

REVISION: The teacher says that the book is poorly written and asks why anyone would buy it.

OR

The teacher says, "The book is poorly written. Why would anyone buy it?"

PRACTICE EXERCISE ON CONSISTENCY

DIRECTIONS: Examine each of the following sentences. Make any revisions that will improve consistency. Look for errors involving parallelism, tense, voice, person of pronoun, and direct and indirect discourse.

1. We left after breakfast; then I find an ideal place for a picnic.

2. In felling a tree a good woodsman first cuts a deep notch. Then you saw on the other side of the tree.

3. All play and not working can become tiresome.

4. I bought my ticket and I am waiting for the bus.

5. Our team played the game well, but still the game was not won by them.

6. The policeman said that we could cross the street, but wait until the light is green.

7. If I would have arrived earlier, I would have been on time.

8. A teacher is always pleased when you laugh at their jokes.

9. The new employee soon proved himself to be not only capable but also a man who could be trusted.

10. Bill signed up for a course in typing, and a typewriter was purchased by him.

ANSWERS:

1. Tense Inconsistency.

   Correction: We left after breakfast; then I <u>found</u> an ideal place for a picnic.

2. Person of Pronoun Inconsistency.

   Correction: In felling a tree a good woodsman first cuts a deep notch. Then <u>he saws</u> on the other side of the tree.

3. Faulty Parallelism.

   Correction: All play and <u>no work</u> can become tiresome.

4. Tense Inconsistency.

   Correction: I <u>have bought</u> my ticket and I am waiting for the bus.

5. Shift in Voice.

   Correction: Our team played the game well but <u>still</u> <u>lost</u>.

6. Shift in Discourse.

   Correction: The policeman said that we could cross the street <u>after the light turned green</u>.

7. Tense Inconsistency.

   Correction: If I <u>had arrived</u> earlier, I would have been on time.

8. Pronoun Shift. (Singular to Plural)

   Correction: A teacher is always pleased when you laugh at <u>his</u> jokes.

9. Faulty Parallelism.

   Correction: The new employee soon proved himself to be not only capable but <u>also trustworthy</u>.

10. Shift in Voice.

    Correction: Bill signed up for a course in typing and <u>purchased a typewriter</u>.

NOTE: It is not important that you be able to name the error in sentences like those in the exercise above. However, it is important that you be able to recognize that there is a better way of phrasing each one. If you had any problems, review the appropriate section of the text.

Rules On Agreement

RULE #1   **A SINGULAR SUBJECT REQUIRES A SINGULAR VERB. A PLURAL SUBJECT REQUIRES A PLURAL VERB.**

Notice how we conjugate a verb in the present tense.

SINGULAR	PLURAL
I walk	we walk
You walk	you walk
he walks	they walk

We would never say "They walks to school." We automatically learn to make a verb agree with its subject.

However, we need to examine some instances where this agreement is not as automatic.

EXAMPLE: There (is, are) several ways to solve that problem.

HINT: When   an expression, such as <u>here</u> or <u>there</u> begins a sentence, look for the real subject to appear later. It helps to turn the sentence around to natural order.

REWRITTEN SENTENCE:

Several <u>ways</u> to solve a problem (<u>are</u>, is) there.

(subject)   (verb)

The subject is <u>ways</u>. The verb needed is <u>are</u>.

CORRECTLY WRITTEN:

There <u>are</u> several ways to solve that problem.

EXAMPLE: A box of pencils (is, are) on the table.

HINT: Disregard any prepositional phrases which come between the subject and the verb in a sentence. In many cases these are <u>of phrases</u> such as <u>of pencils</u> above.

REWRITTEN SENTENCE:

A <u>box</u> (of pencils) <u>is</u> on the table.

   ↑   ↑

   (subject)   (verb)

EXAMPLE: Tom, <u>as well as his sister</u>, <u>is</u> coming.

 (subject)   ↑   (verb)

    (interrupting phrase)

The same principle applies here. The interrupting phrase does not affect the number of the verb.

RULE #2 A COMPOUND SUBJECT CONNECTED BY <u>AND</u> REQUIRES A PLURAL VERB.

EXAMPLE: His study and preparation for the test (was, were) not sufficient.

  compound subject - <u>study and preparation</u>

  require the plural verb - <u>were</u>

REWRITTEN: His study and preparation for the test <u>were</u> not sufficient.

EXAMPLE: Mary and Sue (are, is) here.

  compound subject - <u>Mary and Sue</u>

  require the plural verb - <u>are</u>

REWRITTEN: Mary and Sue <u>are</u> here.

EXCEPTION: In rare instances a compound subject is regarded as a single entity. In such cases it takes a singular verb.

EXAMPLE: Spaghetti and meatballs (is, are) my favorite dish.

spaghetti and meatballs - considered a single item, needs single verb is

REWRITTEN: Spaghetti and meatballs is my favorite dish.

RULE #3   SINGULAR SUBJECTS CONNECTED BY OR OR NOR REQUIRE A SINGULAR VERB.

EXAMPLE: Either John or Mary (is, are) lying.

The singular subjects John and Mary are connected by or and need a singular verb.

REWRITTEN: Either John or Mary is lying.

RULE #4   IF ONE OF THE SUBJECTS CONNECTED BY OR OR NOR IS SINGULAR AND ONE IS PLURAL, THE VERB AGREES WITH THE ONE CLOSER TO IT.

EXAMPLE: Neither my aunts nor Mary (is, are) leaving.

The subject closer to the verb is Mary.

Because Mary is singular, you use the singular verb form, is.

REWRITTEN: Neither my aunts nor Mary is leaving.

EXAMPLE: Neither Mary nor my aunts (is, are) leaving.

The subject closer to the verb is aunts.

Because aunts is plural, you use the plural verb form, are.

REWRITTEN: Neither Mary nor my aunts are leaving.

RULE #5   SUBJECTS THAT ARE SINGULAR IN MEANING BUT PLURAL IN FORM (NEWS, ECONOMICS, MEASLES, ETC.) REQUIRE A SINGULAR VERB.

EXAMPLE: Mathematics (is, are) my favorite subject.

Mathematics is plural in form, but singular in meaning and requires the singular verb form, is.

REWRITTEN: Mathematics is my favorite subject.

RULE #6   MAKE A PRONOUN AGREE WITH ITS ANTECEDENT. (THE NOUN OR PRONOUN IT REFERS TO).

REMEMBER: anyone, everyone, someone, etc., are considered singular and take the masculine singular pronoun.

EXAMPLE: If anyone is late, refer (him, them) to me.

Anyone is singular and requires the singular pronoun, him.

REWRITTEN: If anyone is late, refer him to me.

PRACTICE ON AGREEMENT

DIRECTIONS: Choose the correct verb form.

1. There, writhing in the grass, (was, were) four snakes.

2. Each of the girls (is, are) presenting a gift.

3. Macbeth himself, rather than the witches, (was, were) responsible for his downfall.

4. Interesting news (is, are) what sells papers.

5. Will everyone please open (his, their) book to the first chapter?

6. A magazine and a newspaper (was, were) lying on the table.

7. Either your mother or your father (is, are) required to sign the report card.

8. (Is, Are) each of cakes the same size?

9. A bushel of apples (cost, costs) a dollar.

10. Either Mary or the boys (was, were) late.

ANSWERS:

1. were   Subject is <u>four snakes</u>.

2. is   Subject is <u>each</u>. Disregard the prepositional phrase <u>of the girls</u>.

3. was   Subject is <u>Macbeth</u>. Disregard the intervening phrase.

4. is   Subject is <u>news</u>, a singular noun that looks plural.

5. his   <u>Everyone</u> is singular and always takes the masculine singular pronoun.

6. were   Subject is compound: <u>magazine and newspaper</u>. Plural verb is needed.

7. is   <u>Mother</u> or <u>father</u> = two singular subjects connected by <u>or</u> and need a singular verb.

8. Is   Subject is <u>each</u> which needs a singular verb.

9. costs   Subject is <u>bushel</u> which is singular.

10. were   <u>Mary or the boys</u> = subject. One is singular; the other plural. Verb agrees with word closer to it.

Practice With CLEP English Composition Examination Type Questions

Now that you have reviewed some of the material you will need to know in order to perform well on a test of standard written English, it's time to examine the types of questions you will encounter on the CLEP General English Composition Examination.

There are three types of questions presented in Section I of both the all multiple choice version and the version with essay. The following section will help you analyze and become familiar with each type.

CLEP QUESTION TYPE #1

This type of question asks you to identify wording that is ambiguous or unclear or that does not follow the rules of standard written English.

Four parts of the sentence are underlined. You are to select the part that must be changed in order to make the sentence correct. If there is no error you select answer E.

Here is a sample question:

The tall woman <u>strode confidently</u> <u>into the room</u> and <u>announces</u>, "I <u>am</u>
              A   B   C   D
Mrs. Jones, your new teacher." <u>No error</u>
                                    E

Answer to sample question: The answer is C. The problem is an unnecessary shift in tense. Since the first verb in the sentence is past tense (<u>strode</u>), <u>announces</u> (present tense) should be <u>announced</u> (past tense). Note that <u>am</u>, although present tense, is correct because it is part of a direct quotation.

You will find the following procedure helpful when you work with this type of question:

1. Read the entire sentence carefully. Make sure you understand it.

2. Assume that the elements that are **not underlined are correct and cannot be changed**.

3. Remember errors can be in many different areas. Some common problems to consider are the following:

> parallel structure
> correct usage
> idiomatic use of language
> appropriate verb tense
> clarity of expression
> elimination of wordiness and redundancy
> agreement between parts of the sentence
> (subject-predicate verb, pronoun-antecedent)

4. All you have to do is find the error. **You do not have to analyze it or correct it**.

PRACTICE - CLEP QUESTIONS, TYPE #1

DIRECTIONS: The following sentences contain problems in grammar, usage, diction (choice of words) and idiom. Some sentences are correct. No sentence contains more than one error. You will find that the error, if there is one, is underlined and lettered. Assume that elements of the sentence that are not underlined are correct and cannot be changed. In choosing answers, follow the requirements of standard written English.

If there is an error, select the <u>one underlined part</u> that must be changed to make the sentence correct and blacken the corresponding space on your answer sheet.

If there is no error, select answer (E).

1. Because <u>only</u> a small part of the former number of species still <u>exist</u>,
           A   B
    scientists <u>must study</u> many extinct reptiles <u>by examining</u> fossils and
                    C   D
    footprints. <u>No error</u>
                     E

2. <u>After learning</u> about Mark Twain's <u>varied and interesting</u> life, I <u>could not</u>
          A   B   C
    <u>hardly</u> wait <u>to read</u> one of his novels. <u>No error</u>
        C   D   E

3. <u>According to</u> the instructions <u>printed on</u> the course guide, the purpose of
          A   B
    the paper <u>will be</u> to enumerate the causes of the war and <u>what were</u> the
                  C   D
    results. <u>No error</u>
                  E

4   By the time the artist <u>moved</u> to Paris, his work <u>had evolved</u> from realism
                              A   B
    into a <u>so-called</u> Blue Period in which he painted figures <u>in various shades</u>
                C   D
    of blue. <u>No error</u>
                  E

5. Each of the potential contestants <u>was ushered</u> into the room and then
                                            A

   <u>confronted</u> by an interviewer <u>who wanted</u> to know about <u>their</u> most
        B   C   D

   interesting experience. <u>No error</u>
                               E

ANSWERS:

1. (B)   The singular verb <u>exists</u> is needed to agree with the singular
         subject <u>part</u>. <u>Of the former number of species</u> is a prepositional
         phrase and has no bearing on the number of the verb.

2. (C)   <u>Could not hardly</u> is ungrammatical. It should be <u>could hardly</u>.

3. (D)   <u>What were</u> makes the sentence awkward and the construction
         nonparallel. The phrase should be eliminated from the sentence.

4. (E)   No error.

5. (D)   The sentence is speaking of each contestant as an individual.
         Notice that the verb <u>was ushered</u> should be singular in order to
         agree with the subject <u>each</u>. The pronoun, therefore, should be <u>his</u>.

NOTE: On the actual CLEP English Composition Examination, you will not
need to give the reason why you chose a particular answer.

CLEP QUESTION TYPE #2

In this type of question all or part of the sentence will be underlined. Below
each sentence are five ways of phrasing the underlined parts. You are to select
the answer that produces the most effective sentence. You want to choose the
one that is clear and exact, without awkwardness or ambiguity. You are to
follow the requirements of standard written English.

Answer (A) is <u>always</u> the same as the underlined part. You should choose (A) if
you think that the original sentence needs no revision.

In working with this type of question you will be using all the things you have
learned so far. You should consider such things as correct tense sequence,
agreement between parts of the sentence, correct sentence joining, parallelism,
idiom, redundancy, and any of the other areas mentioned so far in this book.

SAMPLE QUESTION:

Underline: Sometimes the question is the reason of obeying orders, not which order to obey.

(A) Sometimes the question is the reason of obeying orders
(B) The question sometimes is of why orders are obeyed
(C) The question sometimes relates to the reason to obey orders
(D) Sometimes the question is in the nature of why orders are taken
(E) Sometimes the question is why we obey orders

The best way to approach this question is to first make sure that you understand the original sentence. Remember, you are not to change the meaning. Next, examine each revision and substitute each for the underlined part of the original.

The best answer to the sample question is (E). All other choices are either awkward (they do not fit into the natural rhythm of English speech) or wordy (too many unnecessary words or redundancy). Notice how straight-forward and uncluttered choice (E) is.

PRACTICE - CLEP QUESTIONS, TYPE #2

DIRECTIONS: In each of the following sentences, some part or all of the sentence is underlined. Below each sentence you will find five ways of phrasing the underlined part. Select the answer that produces the most effective sentence, one that is clear and exact, without awkwardness or ambiguity. In choosing answers, follow the requirements of standard written English. Choose the answer that best expresses the meaning of the original sentence.

Answer (A) is always the same as the underlined part. Choose answer (A) if you think the original sentence needs no revision.

1. The men were tired, but they work hard all day.

    (A) but they work hard all day
    (B) because they had worked hard all day
    (C) when they worked hard all day
    (D) who were working hard all day
    (E) and they had worked hard all day

2. The more I thought about my sick friend, <u>the sadder I felt</u>.

   (A) the sadder I felt
   (B) the more I felt sadly
   (C) the more sadly I felt
   (D) I felt increasingly sadder
   (E) increasingly I felt sadly

3. Because of his rowdy behavior, John was <u>arrested; they had taken him to jail</u>.

   (A) arrested; they had taken him to jail
   (B) arrested and they took him to jail
   (C) arrested, and he had been taken to jail
   (D) arrested and taken to jail
   (E) arrested, being taken to jail

4. <u>His failure to realize that his teasing was offensive was the cause why Bill was generally unpopular</u>.

   (A) His failure to realize that his teasing was offensive was the cause why Bill was generally unpopular.
   (B) Not realizing that his teasing was offensive, Bill was unpopular.
   (C) Bill was generally unpopular because he failed to realize that his teasing was offensive.
   (D) Bill did not realize his teasing was offensive causing his unpopularity.
   (E) Bill did not realize his teasing was offensive insofar as he was caused to be unpopular.

ANSWERS:

1. (B) What is needed is a conjunction that shows the correct relationship between the two ideas. The men were tired <u>because</u> they had worked. Also, <u>had worked</u> is needed (<u>past perfect</u>) because the <u>working</u> came before the <u>being tired</u>.

2. (A) Answer (A) is the simplest, most direct way to make the statement. It also maintains parallelism (<u>the more I thought</u> ... <u>the sadder I felt</u>). (B), (C), and (E) contain a grammatical error. You feel <u>sad</u>, not <u>sadly</u>. <u>Feel</u> is a linking verb and is not modified by an adverb. (D) is not parallel.

3. (D) Answers (A) and (B) contain the general pronoun <u>they</u> with no antecedent. (C) is wordy. (E) is awkward.

4. (C) (A) <u>cause why</u> is not idiomatic. (B) slightly changes the meaning. (D) <u>causing his unpopularity</u> is a dangling modifier. (E) unnecessarily uses the passive (<u>he was caused</u>) and is awkward and wordy.

CLEP QUESTION TYPE #3

This type of question provides you with an early draft of a student essay in which the sentences have been numbered for easy reference. Some parts of the selection need to be changed.

The question is designed to test your ability to improve sentence structure and word choice. Some questions refer to the entire essay and ask you to consider organization, development, and effectiveness of language in relation to the author's purpose and intended audience.

The best way to approach the question is to read the entire selection carefully, making note of the author's purpose and audience which is stated before the selection. Then read and answer each question, referring back to the selection as necessary.

DIRECTIONS: Each of the following selections is an early draft of a student essay in which the sentences have been numbered for easy reference. Some parts of the selections need to be changed.

Read each selection and then answer the questions that follow. Some questions are about particular sentences or parts of sentences and ask you to improve sentence structure and diction (word choice). In making these decisions, follow the conventions of standard written English. Other questions refer to the entire essay or parts of the essay and ask you to consider organization, development, and effectiveness of language in relation to purpose and audience. After you choose each answer, fill in the corresponding oval on your answer sheet.

Questions 1-3 are based on the following first draft of a student essay.

(1) The book <u>To Kill a Mockingbird</u>, by Harper Lee, should be added to the required reading list at our high school. (2) Some students already do read this fine book. (3) Many more would do so if it were added to the curriculum.

(4) It is, first of all, a good story that holds my interest. (5) The first person narrator, a young girl named Scout, draws the reader in and makes him feel part of the story. (6) The reader sees everything through her eyes. (7) Most importantly, the theme of the book is the evil of racial discrimination, or for that matter of any kind of prejudice. (8) The trial of Tom Robinson and the persecution of Boo Radley are two major plot elements that bring out this theme.

(9) These are just a few of the reasons that I feel this modern Pulitzer Prize winning book should be part of our literature curriculum.

1. Which of the following would be the best way to revise and combine sentences 2 and 3 (reproduced below)?

   Some students already do read this fine book. Many more would do so if it were added to the curriculum.

   (A) If added to the curriculum, many more students would read this book.
   (B) While some students already do read this fine book, many more would do so if it were added to the curriculum.
   (C) Some students already read this fine book, many more would do so if it were added to the curriculum.
   (D) Many more students than a few would read this fine book if it were added to the curriculum.
   (E) The book would have been read by more students if it had been added to the curriculum.

2. Which of the following sentences, if added after sentence 3, would best link the first paragraph with the rest of the essay?

   (A) I think that everyone should read this book.
   (B) This is one of the best books I have ever read.
   (C) This is a much better book than some of the others that are currently required reading.
   (D) There are several reasons that this book is a valuable reading experience for students.
   (E) Many teachers agree with this idea.

3. All of the following strategies are used by the writer of this passage **EXCEPT**:

   (A) backing up the main idea with reasons
   (B) selecting specific examples
   (C) ordering reasons from least to most important
   (D) building suspense
   (E) restating the main idea in the conclusion

ANSWERS

1. (B) This answer smoothly and correctly combines the two sentences, showing the correct relationship between the two ideas. Answer (A) begins with a dangling modifier. (C) is a run-on sentence. Choice (D) is awkwardly worded. (E) uses an unnecessary switch to passive voice and switches tenses.

2. (D) This choice states the main idea of the paper and prepares the reader for the reasons that follow.

3. (D) All of the strategies are used except building suspense.

CLEP QUESTION TYPE #4

This type of question appears only in Section II of the all multiple choice test, not in the version with essay.

This type of question will present you with a sentence to be rephrased according to directions. You will begin with a sentence that is acceptable as it stands; however, the revised sentence is meant to be an improvement over the original, or at least equally acceptable.

The question is designed to test your ability to move from coordination to subordination, to change emphasis, to maintain parallel structure, to express ideas clearly by placing modifiers appropriately, to keep verb in agreement with subject, and to use language idiomatically.

SAMPLE QUESTION:

Arriving on the first day of school, he found that the building had been painted.

Substitute He arrived for Arriving.

(A) and had found
(B) and then finding
(C) and there he had found
(D) and so he found
(E) and found

The idea is to mentally revise the sentence, making notes in the test booklet if it helps you. Then examine the phrases in the choices (A) - (E) and find the word or phrase that is included in your revised sentence.

In the example above, the answer is (E). The revised sentence would read:

He arrived on the first day of school and found that the building had been painted.

As you try the sample questions, remember to be sure that you understand the original sentence, revise the sentence mentally or by writing in your book, and then examine the answers for the words that are included in your revision. Examining the answers before you revise the sentence might be confusing.

PRACTICE - CLEP QUESTIONS, TYPE #4

DIRECTIONS: Revise each of the sentences below according to the directions that follow it. Some directions require you to rephrase only part of the original sentence; others require you to recast the entire sentence. You may need to omit or add certain words in constructing an acceptable revision, but you should keep the meaning of your revised sentence as close to the meaning of the original sentence as the directions permit. Your new sentence should follow the conventions of standard written English and should be clear and concise.

Look through answer choices A-E under each question for the exact word or phrase that is included in your revised sentence. If you have thought of a revision that does not include any of the words or phrases listed, try to revise the sentence again so that it does include the wording in one of the answer choices.

1.   The climate of Alaska is typically cold.

Substitute Cold weather for The climate.

(A) typically
(B) in the fashion of
(C) in line with
(D) typical of
(E) in its typicality

2.   Owing to her cheerful personality, Abby has many friends.

Begin with Many people liked.

(A) and
(B) so
(C) while
(D) because
(E) although

3. Wanting to succeed, Mike worked very hard.

    Begin with <u>Mike worked</u>.

    (A) in order for him
    (B) in a hope that
    (C) because he wanted
    (D) for being
    (E) with the result

4. History does not tell us as much of man's nobility as it tells us of his cruelty.

    Change <u>does not tell as much of</u> to <u>tells us far more of</u>.

    (A) rather than
    (B) than
    (C) and not
    (D) than are
    (E) but not

ANSWERS:

1. (D) Cold weather is <u>typical of</u> Alaska.

2. (D) Many people liked Abby <u>because</u> of her cheerful personality.

3. (C) Mike worked very hard <u>because he wanted</u> to succeed.

4. (B) History tells us far more of man's cruelty <u>than</u> of his nobility.

This is one type of question that seems to get easier with practice. There will be more samples later in the book. If you had a great deal of difficulty, it might be a good idea to rewrite the sentence instead of revising it in your mind. However, remember that this takes more time, so try to use any type of shorthand that you will be able to transcribe.

Let us continue our review of skills needed for the CLEP General English Composition Examination.

The Paragraph

A paragraph is a series of sentences developing one topic. It states a point and then develops it. It also serves as a division the reader can see, breaking up the monotony of a page of print.

Many of the skills involved in constructing a good paragraph can be applied to writing a good theme or article. A good expository paragraph should have a topic sentence, unity, coherence, and sufficient development. We will examine how to attain each of these qualities.

1. THE TOPIC SENTENCE

A well-written paragraph usually has one central thought, and this thought is often stated in one sentence called the topic sentence. The topic sentence is frequently the first sentence in the paragraph, although it may be placed anywhere. The inexperienced writer should stick to placing it at the beginning.

Here are two examples of brief paragraphs. Find the topic sentence (main idea) in each.

A

One of the biggest problems in American education is a result of faulty communication. Teachers complain that administrators object to new ideas. Administrators complain that their teachers won't experiment with new techniques. Students complain that no one will listen to their point of view, while administrators and teachers claim that the students are too apathetic to have a point of view. When will all these inter-dependent cogs in the educational wheel start listening to each other?

B

The sky was overcast as I left my home at 6 AM. The wind began to pick up, rocking my compact car from side to side as I drove along the deserted road. Animals scurried for shelter as gigantic raindrops began to pelt the car window. The whir of the windshield wipers drowned out the voice on the radio. Another wet, depressing Monday morning was under way.

ANSWERS:

Paragraph A: The topic sentence is the first sentence.

Paragraph B: The topic sentence is the last sentence.

2. UNITY

In a unified paragraph, every sentence relates to the topic sentence. In order to test a paragraph for unity, find the topic sentence; then read each sentence and check to see that it relates directly to the topic sentence. If it is even slightly off the subject, it will destroy the unity of the paragraph.

Read the paragraph below. Decide whether it is unified. If it is not unified, what sentence or sentences would you eliminate to improve it?

> Although they have been told over and over that speed is a major cause of traffic accidents, many drivers continue racing toward death on the highways. Rather than miss the opening scene of a film or keep Grandmother's Sunday dinner waiting, drivers exceed the fifty-five mile limit, pass on steep hills, and squeal around sharp curves. Newspapers are filled with gory details of mangled bodies in wrecks caused by bad road conditions, faulty equipment, or drunken drivers. Just look at the number of cars Detroit must recall every year because of manufacturing defects. A speeder is someone who gambles that he will not become a statistic. He is a menace who must make good time on the road even though he is risking his own life and endangering the lives of those who must drive on the same roadways.

ANSWER:

There are two sentences that do not belong in this paragraph. The first sentence, the topic sentence, establishes that the writer is going to discuss speed as a cause of accidents. Therefore, the sentences: "Newspapers are filled with gory details...drivers." and "Just look at...manufacturing defects." should be eliminated. Although they relate to accidents, they are off the topic of speed and destroy the unity of the paragraph.

3. COHERENCE

When we speak of coherence, we are referring to that quality that makes writing hold together. The sentences of a paragraph have coherence if they flow smoothly, naturally, and logically from one to another.

One of the best ways to achieve coherence is to present a clear arrangement of ideas. The arrangement of ideas depends on the topic of the paragraph. Three common methods of arranging ideas are chronologically, spatially, and order of importance.

CHRONOLOGICAL ARRANGEMENT (TIME ORDER)

The natural way to tell a story or relate an incident is to give the events in the order that they occurred. Another common situation where chronological arrangement is useful is in telling how to do or make something.

SPATIAL ARRANGEMENT

The natural way to describe objects is by their position in relation to each other, for example, from left to right or top to bottom. Details in a paragraph should be arranged spatially when the writer is describing a room or setting a scene.

ORDER OF IMPORTANCE ARRANGEMENT

In a paragraph presenting facts, ideas, or opinions, details and examples are often arranged in order of their importance. The order may be from least to most important or vice-versa. In general, the former order is preferred, especially in an argumentative paragraph so that the argument may build to a climax.

COHERENCE - SAMPLE PARAGRAPHS

Below are three paragraphs which illustrate the three orders of arranging ideas discussed on the preceding page: chronological, spatial, and order of importance. It should be obvious which order each exemplifies. See if you can identify each.

1

To pot a plant correctly, first hold the plant gently while you put it into the pot, adding enough soil mixture to bring the top of the soil ball to just below the pot's rim. Then rest the plant in the pot with one hand, and using the other to add mixture, fill in around the soil ball. When the mix is at the same level as the base of the stem, press down with your forefinger all around the stem to bring the roots into contact with the mixture.

2

Reading and writing ought to be improved in two ways. The first is to give general knowledge to students in these two areas. That is, to recognize that while Plato and Shakespeare may not have much to do with getting a job, they have a lot to do with raising the quality of thought. More important, special training in reading and writing should be required in all schools and universities. In short, more reading, more homework, and more writing sounds like the best program to me.

3

In the dark hallway we noticed the line of skeletons hanging on the walls to our right and to our left. Water dripped from overhead as the light from the sole window cast eerie shadows on the cement floor. At last, the tour of the ancient castle was coming to an end. We could see the massive wooden doors ahead of us, at the end of the long, dismal corridor.

ANSWERS:

1. Chronological
2. Order of Importance
3. Spatial

4. TRANSITIONS

In a well planned paragraph, sentences follow one another naturally. Sometimes, however, you need to provide clues to help your reader follow your train of thought.

In a single paragraph these clues are usually pronouns which refer to words or ideas in preceding sentences. They carry the reader back to what has just been said.

Another way to keep the thought flowing smoothly is through the use of connectives. Below is a partial list of commonly used connectives. One caution is necessary. Do not overuse these expressions or your writing will be wordy and cumbersome.

SOME TRANSITIONAL EXPRESSIONS

accordingly	at the same time	for example
after	before long	furthermore
afterward	besides	however
also	consequently	in addition
another	even so	later
as a result	finally	moreover
at first	first (second, third)	nevertheless
next	on the other hand	otherwise
thus	similarly	when
soon	yet	then
therefore		

A third way to achieve transition is to repeat a word from a preceding sentence or use a synonym for a word in a preceding sentence.

EXAMPLE:

> Anyone tuning in a radio hears static between stations. The same noise may drown out a distant station altogether. It often makes radio listening more a chore than a pleasure.

In this paragraph <u>noise</u> and <u>it</u> are words used to refer back to static.

PRACTICE WITH TRANSITIONAL EXPRESSIONS

DIRECTIONS: Reread the three sample paragraphs. Underline all the transitional expressions (connectives) that you can find. Then check your answers with the list below.

1

To pot a plant correctly, first hold the plant gently while you put it into the pot, adding enough soil mixture to bring the top of the soil ball to just below the pot's rim. Then rest the plant in the pot with one hand, and using the other to add mixture, fill in around the soil ball. When the mix is at the same level as the base of the stem, press down with your forefinger all around the stem to bring the roots into contact with the mixture.

2

Reading and writing ought to be improved in two ways. The first is to give general knowledge to students in these two areas. That is, to recognize that while Plato and Shakespeare may not have much to do with getting a job, they have a lot to do with raising the quality of thought. More important, special training in reading and writing should be required in all schools and universities. In short, more reading, more homework, and more writing sounds like the best program to me.

3

In the dark hallway we noticed the line of skeletons hanging on the walls to our right and to our left. Water dripped from overhead as the light from the sole window cast eerie shadows on the cement floor. At last, the tour of the ancient castle was coming to an end. We could see the massive wooden doors ahead of us, at the end of the long, dismal corridor.

ANSWERS:

PARAGRAPH #1	PARAGRAPH #2	PARAGRAPH #3
first	first	to our right
then	that is	to our left
when	more important	at last
	in short	

Notice also the repetition of the words <u>plant</u> and <u>pot</u>.

5. METHODS OF DEVELOPMENT

There are several ways of developing a paragraph. By developing we mean expanding or elaborating upon the main idea or topic sentence. This section will examine five ways of developing a paragraph that are useful in expository writing: facts, examples, incident, reasons, comparison and contrast.

FACTS: A fact is something that actually happened and can be proven to be true. If you choose to support an idea with facts, make sure that your facts can be verified and are not merely opinion. For example, you might write a paragraph developing the idea that 1968 was a momentous year by citing the events of that year.

EXAMPLES: Sometimes a topic sentence may be developed by giving one or more examples of the truth it expresses. The topic sentence "Our school has a club to fit everyone's interest," could be developed with examples.

INCIDENT: An incident or brief event may provide an effective means of illustrating the idea expressed in a topic sentence. For example, the topic sentence "Sometimes a pet can seem human," could be developed by a brief story that illustrates the point.

REASONS: Topic sentences often make statements that provoke the question "Why?" In general, the writer who starts with such a statement should give reasons to support it. For example, a paragraph on the subject of why we should have a woman President could be developed with reasons.

COMPARISON
AND CONTRAST: Paragraphs may be developed by comparisons (which show similarities) or by contrasts (which show differences) or by a combination of the two. A special note is needed about the organization of this type of paragraph. It may be done point by point; that is, by making a statement about one thing and comparing or contrasting it immediately with another. For example, comparing and contrasting apples and oranges might go something like this:

	APPLES	**ORANGES**
SHAPE	round (X)	round (Y)
CLASS	fruit (X)	fruit (Y)
COLOR	red, yellow, green (X)	orange (Y)

The paragraph could discuss the shape of apples and then the shape of oranges. The pattern would be XY XY XY.

Another way to organize the same comparison and contrast would be to tell everything about apples and then everything about oranges, in the same order, of course: shape, class, color - shape, class, color. That pattern would be XXX YYY. In longer paragraphs or essays the first method is easier for the reader to follow than the second.

It should be noted that each method of development lends itself to a different method of organization. The special problems involved in organizing a comparison and contrast paragraph have already been discussed. A paragraph developed by incident is probably best arranged chronologically. One developed by examples, facts, or reasons will probably lend itself to order of importance organization.

In summary, you should keep the following things in mind when you are writing or analyzing a paragraph.

1. There should be a clear topic sentence.

2. Each sentence in the paragraph should relate to the topic sentence. (unity)

3. A logical pattern of organizing the ideas and clear transitions between ideas is necessary. (coherence)

4. You should choose the method of development that will best elaborate on your topic sentence. (reasons, facts, etc. the methods may also be used in combination)

ADEQUATE DEVELOPMENT

In developing a paragraph, be sure to supply enough information to explain or support your ideas and to keep your reader interested. Avoid the thinness that results from merely repeating the main idea in different words. Go beyond generalities to specific details. On the next page are two paragraphs on the same topic. One is not adequately developed; the other is. Note the difference in the impression you get from reading each.

1

The world population of tigers has shrunk from about 100,000 at the turn of the century to 4,000 today. This is a drop of about 96,000. At this rate there won't be any tigers left by the year 2000. Tigers will have become extinct. This dramatic drop in population is probably due to their loss of habitat due to human occupation and activities.

2

The world population of tigers has shrunk from about 100,000 at the turn of the century to 4,000 today. Of the eight regional subspecies of tiger, the smallest, the Bali tiger, is extinct. The Caspian tiger, which once ranged from Afghanistan to eastern Turkey, may also be extinct by this time. Only four or five Javan tigers still live in the wild. There are few Chinese tigers still in existence. It is estimated that, in addition to these small numbers, about 2,000 Indochinese tigers and the same number of Indian or Bengal tigers still survive.

Note the difference between the two paragraphs. The first does not really contain very much information after the topic sentence. Most of the paragraph simply rephrases the topic sentence. In contrast, the second paragraph gives many facts and examples to support the main idea. Of the two, the second is much better developed.

CONSTRUCTING A PARAGRAPH

Suppose you were given the topic "Advantages or Disadvantages of Television Courses." How would you go about constructing a paragraph? Think about it before you look at the sample plan and paragraph below. Remember, there are many ways to approach the topic. What you will be looking at is simply one example.

SAMPLE PARAGRAPH PLAN:

TOPIC: Advantages or Disadvantages of a Distance Learning Course

TOPIC SENTENCE: There are several advantages in taking a distance learning course.

METHOD OF DEVELOPMENT: Reasons

METHOD OF ORGANIZATION: Least to most important

MAIN POINTS: Flexibility
Repetition
Comfort

SAMPLE PARAGRAPH

There are several advantages in taking a distance learning course. The first is flexibility. Instead of having a set hour to attend class, a distance learning student may often choose the hour he wishes to study. This point brings up the second advantage, the availability of repetition. In an ordinary class situation, a student must rely on his notes or his memory to review a difficult concept. The distance learning student can often review areas of difficulty multiple times. Perhaps the greatest advantage over the conventional classroom, however, is comfort and informality. No more trudging through snowstorms to get to class. No more hard chairs and uncomfortable positions. In addition, anyone who gets bored, sleepy, or restless can take a break without hurting anyone's feelings.

PARAGRAPH PRACTICE - SCRAMBLED PARAGRAPHS

EXAMPLE #1

DIRECTIONS: The following Sentences, if arranged logically, would form a coherent paragraph. Number them in the order you think they should appear in a paragraph.

_____   First, there is the problem of trying to find things to occupy the little ones for twelve or more hours a day.

_____   Most difficult of all is having the patience and stamina to deal with arguments, boredom, and other problems all day long.

_____   While summer may be the favorite season of children, it certainly causes problems for parents.

_____   It's no wonder many mothers and fathers breathe a sigh of relief when the school bell rings in September.

_____   Also, there is the difficulty of rearranging parent activities or work schedules or of finding child care when schedules cannot be rearranged.

ANSWER: 2, 4, 1, 5, 3. The paragraph would read as follows:

While summer may be the favorite season of children, it certainly causes problems for parents. First, there is the problem of trying to find things to occupy the little ones for twelve or more hours a day. Also, there is the difficulty of rearranging parent activities or work schedules or of finding child care when schedules cannot be rearranged. Most difficult of all is having the patience and stamina to deal with arguments, boredom, and other problems all day long. It's no wonder many mothers and fathers breathe a sigh of relief when the school bell rings in September.

Notice that the paragraph begins with a topic sentence. The words <u>first</u>, <u>also</u>, and <u>most difficult of all</u> are clues to the order in which the sentences should be arranged. The last sentence is a good concluding statement.

EXAMPLE #2

DIRECTIONS: Follow the same directions as you did for the first example, with one addition: this time there is a sentence that does not belong in the paragraph at all. Put an X on the blank in front of it.

_____   If you follow all of these hints, you are sure to have money left over in your shopping budget.

_____   Being a careful grocery shopper requires preparation, organization, and self-discipline.

_____   Some checkers work more efficiently than others.

_____   When you arrive at the store, try to stick to your list, unless, of course, you spot something that you need to buy but forgot to write on your list.

_____   Before you even visit the store, you should consult the weekly food ads in your local paper.

_____   Then make a shopping list based on the advertised specials.

_____   Have scissors handy to clip out any useful coupons or special offers.

ANSWER: 6, 1, X, 5, 2, 4, 3. The paragraph is arranged in time order and should read as follows:

Being a careful grocery shopper requires preparation, organization, and self discipline. Before you even visit the store, you should consult the weekly food ads in your local paper. Have scissors handy to clip out any useful coupons or special offers. Then make a shopping list based on the advertised specials. When you arrive at the store, try to stick to your list, unless, of course, you spot something that you need to buy but forgot to write on your list. If you follow all of these hints, you are sure to have money left over in your shopping budget.

CLEP QUESTION TYPE #5

This type of question appears only in Section II of the all multiple-choice version.

Two prose passages written in very different styles are presented. You will be asked questions about the writer's purpose and strategies. The question is designed to test your knowledge of the characteristics of prose that are important to good writing. Some examples are recognition of main idea, author's tone and purpose, positioning of ideas, and general and specific support.

The best way to approach this type of question is to read the passage carefully making sure you understand what the writer is trying to communicate. Then read each question and all the choices for the answer, referring back to the passage as necessary to make the best choice.

PRACTICE - CLEP QUESTION, TYPE #5

DIRECTIONS: Each of the following passages consists of numbered sentences. Because the passages are part of longer writing samples, they do not necessarily constitute a complete discussion of the issues presented.

Read each passage carefully and answer the questions that follow it. The questions test your awareness of a writer's purpose and of characteristics of prose that are important to good writing.

Questions 1-4 refer to the following passage:

(1) I awoke the next morning in our sleeping compartment of the train to the cry of "Snow!" from the bunk above. (2) We scurried to the window to watch the thick, white flakes falling on the already deeply covered fields and houses. (3) My family and I were in Switzerland now, enroute to Austria, and the view out the window looked like the Christmas cards I had mailed out a few days before. (4) We ate our continental breakfast marveling at the scenery. (5) Just before lunch we arrived at our destination, Innsbruck.

(6) Innsbruck is a small city surrounded by the Austrian Alps. (7) It's in the area known as the Tyrol. (8) From our hotel room in the center of town, we had a view of the snow-covered Alps, including the Olympic ski jump. (9) It was so pretty, I could have stayed in the room all day just looking out the window! (10) Since it was the day after Christmas, a holiday in Austria, almost everything was closed. (11) It continued to snow all day, and we

walked around enjoying all the quaint Christmas decorations, including a large tree in front of the thirteenth century town hall. (12) That evening we sampled our first Austrian food in a restaurant that our guide book described as "a rabbit warren of rooms in a thirteenth century building, packed with Austriana and 100 percent genuine." (13) It was an experience in dining and culture to be remembered and savored for years to come.

1. Which of the following best describes the function of sentence 1?

    (A) It states the main idea of the passage.
    (B) It introduces the topic and sets the informal tone of the piece.
    (C) It identifies the exact setting of the piece.
    (D) It provides a generalization that will later be developed.
    (E) It provides specific support for a generalization that will follow.

2. This passage would be most likely to appear in

    (A) a geography book
    (B) a tour guide
    (C) a travel magazine
    (D) a ski magazine
    (E) a restaurant guide

3. Which of the following pairs of words best describe the writer's reaction to the experience?

    (A) Dismay and wonder
    (B) Exhaustion and fear
    (C) Disbelief and anticipation
    (D) Excitement and nervousness
    (E) Wonder and delight

4. Which of the following best describes the purpose of the quote in sentence 12?

    (A) It provides a generalization about Austrian restaurants.
    (B) It uses an outside source to refute the author's view.
    (C) It uses an outside source to supplement the author's view.
    (D) It concludes the selection.
    (E) It prepares the reader for the next paragraph.

ANSWERS:

1. (B)   The first sentence lets the reader know that the writer is on a train. The details set the tone for the light, descriptive, informal nature of the piece.

2. (C)   This type of descriptive writing would most likely appear in a magazine designed to share the experiences of travelers. It is not technical or factual enough to appear in the other choices.

3. (E)   The author is expressing wonder and delight in his first visit to what he describes as a most picturesque setting.

4. (C)   The quote brings in an outside source to help describe the restaurant.

The Essay

The ability to write an expository essay is essential for any student. Whether or not you plan to take the version of the CLEP English examination that requires an essay, you should review this section of the book. For one thing, it will review and synthesize all the skills you have been working on so far by requiring you to put them all together into a final product. Another benefit will be to prepare you for the type of multiple-choice question that asks you to organize material into paragraphs (another aspect of Question Type #4).

The key to writing well is the ability to organize. Organization skill is especially important to a time pressure situation like an essay examination. Let us approach the process of answering the CLEP essay step by step.

STEP #1 READ THE QUESTION AND THE DIRECTIONS CAREFULLY GET STARTED RIGHT AWAY

You will be required to write on a given topic. It will already be limited enough to cover in this type of writing situation. The question will also be general enough for everyone to have some opinion, information, or experience upon which to base an essay. Remember that your tone will be serious. This is an expository exercise, not a creative one. However, you want to make your writing as interesting and alive as possible.

Here is a sample of the kind of question you might encounter:

SAMPLE CLEP ESSAY

DIRECTIONS: You will have 45 minutes to plan and write an essay on the topic specified. You will probably find it best to spend a little time considering the topic and organizing your thoughts before you begin writing. Do not write on a topic other than the one specified.

Take care to express your thoughts on the topic clearly and exactly and to make them of interest. Be specific, using supporting examples whenever appropriate. How well you write is much more important than how much you write.

Write in the answer booklet provided. You may use this booklet for any notes you wish to make before you begin writing.

ASSIGNMENT: Some people believe that too many high school students receive diplomas without having mastered basic skills in reading, mathematics and social sciences. Some states have already adopted a policy by which a student must pass a standardized test in these areas in order to be graduated with his class.

Write an essay in which you support or refute the proposition that all twelfth graders should be required to pass a standardized examination on basic skills before they are given a diploma. Be sure to give reasons for your opinion and to support those reasons with specific examples from your reading or experience.

Have you read the directions carefully? It is a good idea to underline key points both in the directions and the question. Notice that a general statement is made about skills before the question about testing is posed. You are not to write about the lack of basic skills. Your focus is on whether or not a test should be given. If you fully understand the directions and the question, it is time to go on to Step #2.

STEP #2 MAKE A VERY QUICK, VERY SKETCHY OUTLINE

Decide what your point of view will be. This will be the thesis statement that you are going to support. Think of three key points of support for your thesis. If you have time as you begin writing, you may include more, but thinking of three will let you know where you are going. If well-supported, three main points might be all you are able to handle in 45 minutes, and they should sufficiently develop your topic. Here is a sample of an outline you might construct to answer the sample question.

SAMPLE OUTLINE

THESIS: All twelfth-graders should not be required to pass a standardized examination before they get their diplomas.

REASONS: 1. Standardized tests are not good measuring instruments.

2. Who decides what level goes into the tests?

3. Twelfth grade is too late.

Now you have your thesis and three reasons to support it. In your mind you should also have supporting examples for each reason. Do not take the time to write examples for each reason. You also have your basic plan of organization. Your essay should be organized like this:

PARAGRAPH #1 Introduction and Thesis Statement
PARAGRAPH #2 Reason #1 and Support
PARAGRAPH #3 Reason #2 and Support
PARAGRAPH #4 Reason #3 and Support
PARAGRAPH #5 Conclusion

If you have time to include more reasons and support, they would just go into the body of your theme in additional paragraphs. Remember that every essay must have a beginning, a middle and an ending (introduction, body, and conclusion).

Before you begin, you may also consider the order in which you wish to present your ideas. In the sample outline, the most important objection to the twelfth-grade testing will be saved until last.

STEP #3 WRITE AN INTRODUCTORY PARAGRAPH

One of the most difficult things for many writers is getting started. A good introduction is very important to any piece of writing. First, it is essential to catch the interest of the reader. Second, you must focus his attention, especially in expository writing, on the topic to be discussed and your attitude toward the topic. Some of the problems involved in getting started can be eliminated if you learn some common and effective ways to begin an essay.

STATE YOUR POSITION

The most common way to begin an expository essay is simply to state the main idea and topic of your paper. Using our sample question, here is a possible introduction using this technique:

> Although many students are graduating from high school without a mastery of enough basic skills to be considered literate in today's complex world, requiring them to pass a standardized examination in their senior year is not the solution to the problem. There are several reasons why a test is not the answer.

Notice how the question and your thesis have been combined to create an introduction. Also notice that the word I is not present. It is a good to keep the pronoun I and such words as in my opinion out of expository essays. Write from a general point of view. The reader knows that you are stating an opinion.

WRITE A BRIEF HISTORY OF THE SUBJECT OR GIVE BACKGROUND

Another possible way to begin an essay is to give some background on the subject. Remember that because of time limitations, this information must be very brief.

Here is a sample:

> For years employers have been complaining that our schools are graduating functional illiterates who can barely read or write well enough to fill out a job application. All of the sudden, a standardized test, administered in the twelfth grade, has been put forth as the solution. While the problem is a serious one, a test administered to all seniors before graduation is not the best answer.

Notice how the background statement ends with a statement of the author's thesis. Notice also how the topic is clearly revealed by the introduction. This immediate establishment of topic is essential in answering an essay in a test situation.

ASK QUESTIONS

Another way to immediately involve your reader in your essay is to pose questions that you will answer later in the essay or that reveal the topic. Sample:

> What is the latest solution being posed by educators to the problem of growing illiteracy among high school graduates? Why is this solution not going to succeed?

In this particular example, the writer would have to go on to clearly state the topic and his thesis in a second brief introductory paragraph.

WRITE A BRIEF NARRATIVE

Our final example of ways to begin an essay is to tell a brief story or relate an incident. Remember that this incident must be brief and must obviously relate to the topic. You may, of course, make up an incident to illustrate your point. This technique does have the advantage of adding a dimension of drama to an essay. It also tends to engage the reader if it is well done.

Again, using our sample topic, here is an example of how a writer might employ this technique:

Imagine yourself in this situation. It's one month before graduation. Everything rests upon the test that you must take this morning. No one cares that you didn't sleep last night, that you have butterflies in your stomach, and that you always do poorly on standardized tests. They care even less that you just broke up with your girlfriend and you've had the flu all week.

As in the previous example, the writer will then have to state his thesis and topic in a second brief introductory paragraph.

Now that you know four ways to begin an essay, which should you use? That depends upon which one, in your opinion, best fits the topic given and which you feel most comfortable handling in a stressful writing situation.

STEP #4 COMPOSE THE BODY OF THE ESSAY

If you have planned your essay properly, the format will be already set up for you in the outline. You need to be concerned that you provide specific support for your reasons. Also, beware of faulty reasoning and over-generalizing. Remember that few things are always or never true.

The first reason given in our sample outline might be developed in the following manner. This would be the first paragraph in the body of the essay.

First of all, standardized tests are not the best indication of whether or not a student has mastered basic skills. The tests are only as reliable as their designers and proctors make them. The question is, "Who is qualified to decide what the basic skills required for graduation should be?" The next question is, "How can we be sure the test measures these skills?" Another problem is related to the fact that many educators believe that this type of test discriminates against minority groups. It seems that all these variables would detract from the accuracy of measurement in such an important situation.

Notice the transitional phrase "First of all." It serves as a bridge between the two paragraphs. When you are writing your essay, make sure you have a bridge in each paragraph. Also, notice how the writer has backed up his reason with specific information relating to what is wrong with standardized tests. Notice also, the clincher sentence to reinforce the main point at the end of the paragraph.

STEP #5 WRITE A CONCLUDING PARAGRAPH

After you have sufficiently developed your ideas, you are ready to compose the final paragraph. A good conclusion is important if you wish to leave a strong and final impression on your reader.

An effective conclusion should reinforce the central message of your essay, tie together any loose ends, and make sure expectations that you set up in your introduction have been fulfilled.

Some things to avoid in conclusions are cliché solutions, platitudes, panaceas, and raising of new issues that you are not going to discuss.

As with the introduction, there are several techniques you can learn to help you write an effective conclusion. Let's consider three.

SUMMARIZE WHAT YOU HAVE SAID BY BRIEFLY REVIEWING MAJOR POINTS

Be careful not to go into a lengthy repetition of details. Get to the points that you want to emphasize.

Here is a sample, again using our sample topic:

> While the standardized test of basic skills is the easy answer to the problem of declining student skills, it is not the best answer. The unfairness of allowing the future of an eighteen-year-old to rest on an examination, which may or may not be a reliable measure of his skills, is obvious.

Notice that this brief conclusion simply restates the author's thesis and main objective.

DISCUSS THE FUTURE OF YOUR SUBJECT. MAKE A PREDICTION BASED ON WHAT YOU HAVE STATED

Here is a sample of this type of conclusion:

> In the next few years, educators will have to come to terms with this problem. Hopefully, they will find methods, other than standardized tests, of insuring that their graduates are able to read the diplomas that they receive.

GIVE A SOLUTION TO THE PROBLEM THAT YOU HAVE PRESENTED

Here is a sample of this third type of conclusion:

> While most people agree that something should be done about this problem, the arbitrary nature of basing graduation upon a single test is clear. Perhaps the solution lies in holding students at a grade level until they have mastered minimum skills for that level. Even a series of tests, administered every two or three years after a child has entered school, would be a fairer evaluation of performance.

In a short essay, it is sometimes best just to end with the final idea. You might begin the final paragraph by saying "Last and most important...." However, in a formal situation a definite conclusion will usually enhance the impression made by your writing.

If we take all the pieces of the essay we have been using as an example and put them together, adding the rest of the body, the final product would look like this:

Although many students are graduating from high school without a mastery of enough basic skills to be considered literate in today's complex world, requiring them to pass a standardized examination in their senior year is not the solution to the problem There are several reasons why a test is not the answer.

First of all, standardized tests are not the best indication of whether or not a student has mastered basic skills. The tests are only as reliable as their designers and proctors make them. The question is, "Who is qualified to decide what the basic skills required for graduation should be?" The next question is, "How can we be sure the test measures these skills?" Another problem is related to the fact that many educators believe that this type of test discriminates against minority groups. It seems that all these variables would detract from the accuracy of measurement in such an important situation.

Second is the problem of the test construction itself. Just who is qualified to determine what questions will be asked on such a crucial exam? Should it be teachers? How about principals or curriculum experts? Perhaps future employers or college deans should have input. How many people would be involved and who would make the final decision? The problems involved in this area alone could take years to solve.

Last and most important of all, twelfth grade is too late for such a test. What can a student who is years behind in basic skills do at this point? A summer course or even a repeat of twelfth grade probably won't solve the problem. If a test must be given, it would be fairer to administer a series of tests throughout a student's school years. For example, tests given in fifth, ninth, and twelfth grade would give a student an indication of whether he is up to grade level while there is still time to do something about his weaknesses.

While the standardized test of basic skills is the easy answer to the problem of declining student skills, it is not the best answer. The unfairness of allowing the future of an eighteen-year-old to rest on an examination, which may or may not be a reliable measure of his skills, is obvious.

A WORD ABOUT TITLES

While a title is not absolutely necessary on an essay in a test situation, it does add to the overall impression. Since it is such a simple matter, if you have time, include one.

Although the title is the first thing the reader sees, it is frequently the last thing an author writes. The easiest way to title an essay is to take the main idea and shorten it to key words.

Possible titles for the essay we have been studying would be as follows:

The Problems of Standardized Tests for Seniors

The Unfairness of the Test for Diploma Concept

Why Standardized Tests to Qualify for Diplomas Are Unfair

STEP #6 PROOFREADING AND REVISION

Under ideal conditions, a piece of writing should be put aside for at least one day before it is reread and revised. This distance gives the writer more perspective and objectivity in analyzing the paper for errors, sentence structure, diction, logic of argument, and content. However, in a test situation, this kind of quality revision is obviously not possible.

In the test situation try to leave at least a few minutes to proofread your paper for errors. Although your essay will not be rated on the basis of grammar or spelling errors, too many such mistakes are bound to leave an overall negative impression on the reader.

CHECKLIST FOR A GOOD ESSAY

TITLE (IF YOU HAVE TIME)

The title should accurately suggest what the paper is about.

It should stir up interest in the paper.

It should not be too long.

Do not underline or put quotation marks around your own title.

Do capitalize every important word, as well as the first word, of your title.

INTRODUCTION

Make your introduction independent of the title. No noun or pronoun in the first sentence should refer to the title.

Catch your reader's attention.

Establish the tone of the paper as serious, humorous, etc.

Include a thesis statement.

BODY

Develop your thesis statement.

Arrange your ideas in some logical order.

Use concrete details to support your main points.

Show the connection between sentence and between paragraphs with good transitions.

CONCLUSION

Do not merely restate your opening paragraph.

Leave your reader with the point that you wish to emphasize.

PROOFREAD

If possible, allow some time between the final draft and proofreading.

Examine the paper for the following:

    wordiness
    incorrect diction
    misspelling
    incorrect punctuation
    choppy sentences, stringy sentences
    ambiguity
    lack of transitions

How The Essay Will Be Scored

The method used to score the CLEP essay examination is known as the "holistic" method. Rather than isolating such variables in writing as grammar, organization, content, diction, etc., readers will be asked to read the essay quickly and react on the basis of their total impression. Several different readers will rate each essay, and an average rating will be taken. The time limit and pressure of the writing situation will be taken into consideration. Remember, however, that poor organization will detract from the impression made by any piece of writing. If a reader finds it difficult to understand your ideas, they will not have the impact that they might otherwise have.

Following are three sample essays on the same topic. Read each one and decide whether you would rate it as high, middle, or low. Keep in mind the principles of writing and organization that we have covered.

TOPIC: Many times the mass media refer to well-known personalities as "legends in their own time." In some instances, this description is an exaggeration. However, through the course of American history, many figures have attained a status that could be defined as legendary; that is, their virtues or faults are exaggerated to the point that it is difficult to separate fact from fiction.

What twentieth-century American do you think has the potential of attaining the status of legend in the minds of future generations? Take care to express your thoughts on the topic clearly and exactly, and to make them of interest. Be specific, using supporting examples whenever appropriate. How well you write is more important than how much you write.

I think that Mohammed Ali would make as good a folk hero as any other twentieth-century person. There are several reasons for my opinion.

First, the media have helped him in his pursuit of becoming a legend. He is paid millions just to demonstrate his boxing talents for a few minutes. Just about everything that he does is covered on the news.

Secondly, whenever people talk about sports, his name comes up. He also has the accomplishments to back up his boasts. As World Heavyweight Champion, he has proven his boast that he is "The greatest." He has also done more to renew interest in his sport than any other figure. His colorful personality has made the sport of boxing big business again.

In addition, he is a controversial figure. His draftdodging, marital problems, strange assortment of opponents, and constant boasting have made him one of those personalities that you either love or hate. It's hard to be neutral about Ali.

In American legend, figures such as Davy Crockett and Mike Fink boasted their way into our folklore. Anyone who has heard of Walt Disney knows that Crockett killed a bear when he was only three. Even though the frontier is gone, its larger-than-life boasting, "I can do anything" American spirit is embodied in Mohammed Ali. It is in this tradition that he will become a twentieth-century legendary figure.

SAMPLE B

J.F.K.: A Modern Legendary Hero

In the course of American history, many prominent figures have attained legendary status. Stories about such diverse characters as Abraham Lincoln, Davy Crockett and Wyatt Earp have become part of our national folklore. As individual as these men and other legendary heroes might be in their personalities, accomplishments, and status in American history, they have in common a certain romantic, larger-than-life quality which makes them fit subjects for legends. I believe that the twentieth-century man most likely to join their ranks is John F. Kennedy.

One of the prerequisites for becoming a folklore hero is widespread fame. This fame should be based upon accomplishments far above the ordinary which will provide material for the varying degrees of exaggeration found in legends. John F. Kennedy's glamorous family background, heroic feats on P.T. 109, courageous recovery from injury, spectacular rise to the Presidency, and tragic assassination will provide more than enough material for the legend-makers.

Accomplishments and family alone, however, do not guarantee legendary status. A sometimes intangible aura of romance and excitement is also helpful. The youth, vitality, and glamour of the Kennedy family, and of John in particular, will provide for many stories of the fairy-tale variety.

In addition to these qualities, a folklore hero should have a unique philosophy or ideal with which he can be associated. There is often a nickname, such as "Honest Abe," a description, such as "King of the Wild Frontier," or a concept, such as, law and order, which is associated with the character. In the case of John Kennedy, this symbolic association could turn out to be his identification with Camelot or his inaugural plea to "Ask not what your country can do for you, but what you can do for your country."

If further evidence of John Kennedy's qualification for legendary status is needed, one needs only to examine the body of material which has been printed since the assassination; it is emotional and inspiring, rather than analytic and objective. The Kennedy name itself is enough to win a place on the front page of a newspaper or even consideration for a Presidential nomination. This tendency to idealize the man, and everyone associated with him, might be considered as the first stage in the creation of the legend of John F. Kennedy.

I feel that Elvis Presley could become a folk hero. Although he is dead, he could definitely still become one for many reasons.

The first reason that I believe so is because most folk heroes are well-known, such as Elvis was and is still. Look at all the television specials there are about him and all the people that keep visiting his grave and buying souvenirs.

Another reason is that they had to do something famous. Elvis was very famous for his singing. To almost all people he was the greatest. He started a new style of music, and parents hated him.

The last, but not least, reason was most folk heroes get killed. Elvis was sort of killed by himself. He did not have a happy life even though he was so rich and famous. This is true of many famous people.

Even though he is now gone, he will definitely be remembered and imitated. Like all folk heroes, many stories about him are exaggerated, and it's hard to say what he really was like. He is the person whom I think will become a folk hero from the twentieth century.

Now, rate the three essays. Which would you give the rating HIGH, MIDDLE, OR LOW? There should be one with each rating.

Here is how several teachers of writing rated the essays:

ESSAY A - middle
ESSAY B - high
ESSAY C - low

If you examine the essays closely, using guidelines set up in the section on essay writing, you should be able to specifically state the reasons that B is superior to the other two. However, just reading the three quickly, using the "holistic" method should bring you to the same conclusion. The principles of constructing a good essay are essential for the writer, but as a reader, you should be able to pick out a piece of good writing simply by reading and reacting to it.

WRITING YOUR SAMPLE ESSAY

Now that you have completed your review of how to write an essay and learned how it will be scored, you are ready to put it all together and write your own sample essay. Following is a practice question complete with directions. The directions are the same as those you will have when you take the actual CLEP General English Examination with Essay.

It is important to get an accurate idea of how well you write in a test situation; write your sample essay under the same conditions you will encounter on the test day. Assemble all materials before you start. You will need the following:

A.   Several sheets of lined paper.

B.   Two or more ball point pens.

C.   A timer of some kind.

D.   A quiet place where you will not be interrupted.

Do not read the question until you set the timer. Allow yourself only 45 minutes. Check periodically to see how much time you have left so that you will not be forced to stop in the middle of a paragraph. **Do not** quit until 45 minutes have passed!

When you have finished, you will need some feedback on your essay. You could read it yourself and try to evaluate it against the checklist on page 83 of this book. A better evaluation would be to let others read it and give you an opinion. Perhaps you know a teacher of writing who would read and evaluate it.

SAMPLE ESSAY TEST

DIRECTIONS: You will have 45 minutes to plan and write an essay on the topic specified. Read the topic carefully. You are expected to spend a few moments considering the topic and organizing your thoughts before you begin writing. Do not write on a topic other than the one specified. An essay on a topic of your own choice is not acceptable.

The essay is intended to give you an opportunity to demonstrate your ability to write effectively. Take care to express your thoughts on the topic clearly and to make them of interest to the reader. Be specific; use supporting examples whenever appropriate. Remember that how well you write is much more important than how much you write.

SAMPLE TOPIC: The United States system of public education has been the subject of a great deal of criticism over the last few years. Other nations seem to be doing a better job of educating their citizens to compete in our fast-paced, technologically advanced world.

Many ideas have been put forth to improve our public schools. As a concerned citizen, what ideas would you like to see implemented? What needs to be done in order to make our public schools do a better job of educating our citizens? You may want to draw upon your own educational experiences or those of your children for ideas.

Taking The CLEP Examination In English Composition

Now that you have finished the entire review section, you are ready to take a short practice test. The test follows the format of the CLEP General Examination in English Composition.

It is important that you take this test now. While you may have done well on each type of question in isolation in the preceding section of the book, another skill is necessary. You must practice working with a variety of questions. In effect, you need to practice "switching gears" or training your mind to go from one type of question to another in a short period of time.

The following procedure should be followed for maximum benefit:

1. Go through the entire 45-minute sample test. Remember the actual exam is twice this length.

2. Check your answers.

3. Review procedures for doing questions if a particular type is giving you trouble.

4. Remember, in the actual exam everyone takes Part I. Everyone who does not choose to take the essay takes Part II.

Short Sample Test

CLEP GENERAL EXAMINATION IN ENGLISH COMPOSITION
SECTION I
(OF BOTH TEST VERSIONS)

Time: 22 minutes   27 questions

DIRECTIONS: The following sentences contain problems in grammar, usage, diction (choice of words) and idiom. Some sentences are correct. No sentence contains more than one error. You will find that the error, if there is one, is underlined and lettered. Assume that elements of the sentence that are not underlined are correct and cannot be changed. In choosing answers, follow the requirements of standard written English.

If there is an error, select the <u>one underlined part</u> that must be changed to make the sentence correct and blacken the corresponding space on your answer sheet.

If there is no error, select answer (E).

1. A beautiful sheep dog, <u>as well as</u> five cats, <u>are</u> going <u>to be</u> in the
                                    A   B   C
    annual pet show at <u>Kymberly's</u> school. <u>No error</u>
                                D   E

2. <u>Although consulting</u> a computer <u>should never take the place</u> of
              A   B
    consulting a doctor, many people <u>find</u> that online medical resources can
                                                      C
    help <u>them</u> to better understand a problem. <u>No error</u>
              D   E

3. <u>In light of the fact</u> that more <u>than</u> two hundred localities <u>have adopted</u>
            A   B   C
    some form of antismoking legislation, it is not surprising there are
    <u>less</u> new smokers now than ever before. <u>No error</u>
      D   E

91

4. <u>Today's</u> high school graduate <u>has</u> several alternatives: finding a job,
    A   B

    <u>attending college</u>, <u>or the armed forces.</u> <u>No error</u>
       C   D   E

5. If a person <u>has</u> to travel from country to country by plane <u>they are</u> bound
           A   B

    <u>to experience</u> the <u>effects</u> of jet lag. <u>No error</u>
      C   D   E

6. After Beowulf slays the monster, he <u>believes</u> that the countryside <u>is</u> safe;
                                  A   B

    <u>however</u>, on the following night the monster's mother <u>came</u> seeking
      C   D

    revenge. <u>No error</u>
            E

7. Although it was foggy, the Statue of Liberty <u>was seen by us</u> as we <u>entered</u>
                                           A   B

    New York Harbor, <u>one of the busiest</u> harbors <u>in the world.</u> <u>No error</u>
                         C   D   E

8. <u>If I had more time</u> and if he <u>was</u> free, we <u>could have</u> visited all the
          A   B   C

    <u>tourist attractions</u> in the city. <u>No error</u>
         D   E

9. The trend away from pesticides and toward more natural method**s**
    <u>of eradicating</u> destructive insects <u>has spawned</u> a number of <u>non-</u>
    <u>chemical</u>
       A   B   C
    <u>alternatives</u> <u>for controlling</u> garden pests. <u>No error</u>
       C   D   E

10. Between you and <u>I</u>, I <u>would rather take</u> a grammar test than <u>solve math</u>
                   A   B   C

    problems or <u>answer history questions.</u> <u>No error</u>
       C   D   E

DIRECTIONS: In each of the following sentences, some part or all of the sentence is underlined. Below each sentence you will find five ways of phrasing the underlined part. Select the answer that produces the most effective sentence, one that is clear and exact without awkwardness or ambiguity. In choosing answers, follow the requirements of standard written English. Choose the answer that best expresses the meaning of the original sentence.

Answer (A) is always the same as the underlined part. Choose answer (A) if you think the original sentence needs no revision.

11. Tigers still exist in some areas of the world, and so are rapidly disappearing.

    (A) , and so are rapidly disappearing.
    (B) . But they are rapidly about to disappear.
    (C) ; however, they are rapidly disappearing.
    (D) since they are rapidly disappearing.
    (E) rapidly disappearing though they may be.

12. Because the computer was not working, it was disconnected and they sent it to be repaired.

    (A) and they sent it
    (B) being sent
    (C) and it had been sent
    (D) and sent
    (E) ; they had sent it

13. On the fence was twelve birds.

    (A) On the fence was twelve birds.
    (B) Twelve birds were perched on the fence.
    (C) Perched were twelve birds on the fence.
    (D) Perched was twelve birds on the fence.
    (E) Were twelve birds on the fence perched?

14. Seeing their teacher, the students immediately concealed the rubber bands.

    (A) Seeing their teacher, the students
    (B) Their teacher being seen by them, the students
    (C) The students, having seen their teacher, they
    (D) When their teacher was seen, they
    (E) Their teacher having been seen by them, the students

15. I have enjoyed the study of mathematics not only because of its challenge but <u>since all business people like its use</u>.

    (A) since all business people like its use
    (B) on account of it is useful in business
    (C) one also does need it in business
    (D) because of its usefulness in business
    (E) to make use of it in business

16. <u>We planned to travel at night, that's how we could avoid traffic</u>.

    (A) We planned to travel at night, that's how we could avoid traffic.
    (B) Wanting to avoid the traffic, we made plans to travel at night.
    (C) Our plans were night travel so that traffic could be avoided.
    (D) Travel plans at night avoid traffic if planned carefully.
    (E) To avoid the traffic, our plans were that we could travel at night.

17. <u>One should always study for tests</u>, or you might fail.

    (A) One should always study for tests,
    (B) They should always study for tests,
    (C) Always study for tests,
    (D) For tests one should always study,
    (E) He should always study for tests,

18. <u>Although Don was a very good student, he</u> did not particularly like school.

    (A) Although Don was a very good student, he
    (B) Don was a very good student, he
    (C) Because Don was a very good student, he
    (D) Being a very good student; Don
    (E) Although having been a very good student, Don

19. I always <u>enjoy to swim, to hike, and to jog</u>.

    (A) enjoy to swim, to hike, and to jog.
    (B) like to swim, hike, and jog.
    (C) enjoy swimming, hiking, and to jog.
    (D) like to swim, hiking, and to jog.
    (E) like to enjoy to swim, to jog, and hiking.

20. People probably enjoy reading mysteries <u>because of this reason they have</u> <u>found a way to escape from the monotonous routine of everyday</u> <u>existence</u>.

(A) because of this reason they have found a way to escape from the monotonous routine of everyday existence.
(B) because of this reason, and they have found a way to escape from the monotonous routine of everyday existence.
(C) because, they have found a way to escape from the monotonous routine of everyday existence.
(D) the reason being because they have found a way to escape from the monotonous routine of everyday life.
(E) because they have found a way to escape from the monotony of their everyday existence.

DIRECTIONS: Each of the following selections is an early draft of a student essay in which the sentences have been numbered for easy reference. Some parts of the selections need to be changed.

Read each selection and then answer the questions that follow. Some questions are about particular sentences or parts of sentences and ask you to improve sentence structure and diction (word choice). In making these decisions, follow the conventions of standard written English. Other questions refer to the entire essay or parts of the essay and ask you to consider organization, development, and effectiveness of language in relation to purpose and audience. After you choose each answer, fill in the corresponding oval on your answer sheet.

Questions 21-27 are based on the following early draft of a letter to the editor of a local newspaper.

(1) Over 400,000 cats were destroyed last year in shelters in our state. (2) Many of these animals had been deliberately abandoned. (3) Some were lost pets whose owners could not be found. (4) What are needed to end this tragedy are laws that will curb breeding and facilitate the identification of lost animals.

(5) A city near San Francisco has approved an identification law that relies on microchips. (6) To do this, the city council approved an ordinance requiring cat owners to have an identification microchip placed under the skin between the shoulder blades of their cats. (7) The encoded pellet, the size of a grain of rice, is read by a scanner. (8) And it costs only about $5 and lasted the life of the cat. (9) I had one placed in each of my cats, Seymour and Delilah. (10) It was quick, easy, and didn't seem to cause them any discomfort.

(11) I am sure that any responsible cat owner would agree to this proposal if made aware of the availability of the microchip. (12) This ordinance could help reunite thousands of lost cats with their owners and substantially reduce the need to euthanize so many animals unnecessarily.

21. Which of the following is the best way to revise the underlined portions of sentences 2 and 3 (reproduced below) so that the two sentences are combined into one?

Many of these animals had been deliberately abandoned. Some were lost pets whose owners could not be found.

(A) abandoned, and some are lost pets
(B) abandoned, so some were lost pets
(C) abandoned, but some were lost pets
(D) abandoned, and some have been lost pets
(E) abandoned, and some pets were lost

22. In the context of the second paragraph, the best phrase to replace "to do this" in sentence 6 is

(A) To accomplish their purpose
(B) To solve the problems
(C) To facilitate the problem
(D) To help find lost cats
(E) To help reunite owners with their cats

23. In the context of the second paragraph, which of the following is the best version of the underlined version of sentence 8 (reproduced below)?

It costs only about $5 and <u>lasted the life of the cat.</u>

(A) lasts the life of the cat.
(B) lasts as long as the cat should live.
(C) lasted as long as the cat did.
(D) lasted throughout the cat's life.
(E) lasts the cat's lives.

24. All of the following strategies are used by the writer of this passage **EXCEPT**

(A) selecting specific examples
(B) citing examples from his own experience
(C) criticizing those whose views differ from his
(D) citing statistics to back up an idea
(E) proposing a solution to the problem

25. In the context of the first paragraph, which is the best way to revise the underlined part of the sentence (reproduced below)?

What are needed to end this tragedy are laws <u>that will curb breeding and facilitate</u> the identification of lost animals.

(A) that will allow breeding to be curbed as well as facilitate
(B) that will not only curb breeding but will also facilitate
(C) that will curb breeding and allow facilitation of
(D) that curbed breeding and facilitated
(E) that had curbed breeding and facilitated

26. Which of the following sentences would be best placed at the beginning of the second paragraph (before sentence 4)?

(A) An example of this type of law has already been passed in California.
(B) There are many examples of such laws.
(C) New laws are being passed every day.
(D) How about this for an example?
(E) California has a lot of laws like this.

27. Which of the following would best replace "And" at the beginning of sentence 8?

   (A) Nevertheless
   (B) Despite this
   (C) Instead
   (D) Furthermore
   (E) But

Time: 23 minutes   23 questions

DIRECTIONS: The following sentences contain problems in grammar, usage, diction (choice of words) and idiom. Some sentences are correct. No sentence contains more than one error. You will find that the error, if there is one, is underlined and lettered. Assume that elements of the sentence that are not underlined are correct and cannot be changed. In choosing answers, follow the requirements of standard written English.

If there is an error, select the one underlined part that must be changed to make the sentence correct and blacken the corresponding space on your answer sheet.

If there is no error, select answer (E).

28.   The other girls and her officially accepted the award their class had won.
           A   B   C   D
      No error.
           E

29.   No one could decide which was the larger of the two pieces of cake.
           A   B   C   D
      No error.
           E

30.   Although ecologists try to protect the environment, there is difficult
                                                            A

      problems raised by the need of industry to use natural resources.
                    B   C   D
      No error.
           E

31.   The book had been laying on the table for weeks, but I hadn't noticed it
                          A   B   C
      there. No error.
           D   E

32. If we <u>would have</u> <u>known</u> how late <u>it was</u>, we <u>might have</u> decided not to go.
        A   B   C   D
<u>No error.</u>
  E

33. <u>Although</u> the dog lover seems <u>indifferent to</u> cats, we could see that <u>he</u>
   A   B   C
also <u>loved</u> felines. <u>No error.</u>
     D   E

DIRECTIONS: Each of the following selections is an early draft of a student essay in which the sentences have been numbered for easy reference. Some parts of the selections need to be changed.

Read each selection and then answer the questions that follow. Some questions are about particular sentences or parts of sentences and ask you to improve sentence structure and diction (word choice). In making these decisions, follow the conventions of standard written English. Other questions refer to the entire essay or parts of the essay and ask you to consider organization, development, and effectiveness of language in relation to purpose and audience. After you choose each answer, fill in the corresponding oval on your answer sheet.

<u>Questions 34-38</u> are based on the following early draft of a student essay.

(1) Being on your own in a foreign country can be intimidating, especially if you aren't very familiar with the language and customs of this new place. (2) If you do a little preparation and keep your cool, it can be one of the most exciting, rewarding experiences you'll ever have. (3) It is also a challenge.

(4) Before you leave home, buy a good guidebook and read as much as you can before your departure and on the plane. (5) Memorize essential phrases in the country's language so that you can politely greet people, ask directions and say, "Thank you." (6) I have found that people will go out of their way to help a tourist who bothers to be polite and who has made an attempt to speak to them in their language (instead of expecting everyone in the world to speak English). (7) Make your first stop be the city's tourist or visitor center. (8) There you can get all kinds of free, up-to-date information, including a map, public transportation schedules, and restaurant and hotel reservations.

(9) Following these simple steps will get you off to a good start on the road to an enjoyable and educational vacation in a foreign country.

34. Which of the following would best be added to the beginning of sentence 2 in the context of the first paragraph?

(A) And,
(B) But,
(C) However,
(D) Furthermore,
(E) In addition,

35. Which of the following is the best way to revise and combine sentences 2 and 3 (reproduced below)?

If you do a little preparation and keep your cool, it can be one of the most exciting, rewarding experiences you'll ever have. It is also a challenge.

(A) If you do a little preparation and keep your cool, it can be one of the most exciting, rewarding and challenging experiences you'll ever have.
(B) If you do a little preparation and keep your cool, this challenging experience will reward and excite you.
(C) If you do a little preparation and keep your cool, it can be one of the most exciting, rewarding experiences you'll ever have; it is also a challenge.
(D) If you do a little preparation and keep your cool, foreign travel can be one of the most exciting, rewarding, and challenging experiences you'll ever have,
(E) If you do a little preparation and keep your cool, you'll be excited, rewarded, and challenged.

36. In the context of paragraph 2, which of the following phrases would best be placed at the beginning of sentence 7 (reproduced below)?

Make your first stop the city's visitor center.

(A) When you arrive at your destination,
(B) When you get there,
(C) Arriving at your destination
(D) At arrival,
(E) When there

37. In the context of the third paragraph, which of the following is the best version of the underlined portion of sentence 9 (reproduced below)?

Following these simple steps will get you off to a good start on the road to an educational and enjoyable vacation in a foreign country.

(A) (As it is now)
(B) If these simple steps are followed by you, you will get off to a good start
(C) A good start will be gotten by your following these simple steps
(D) While you follow these simple steps, you will get off to a good start
(E) These simple steps will get you off to a good start if followed

38. The writer of the passage could best improve the second paragraph by

(A) acknowledging drawbacks to suggestions
(B) eliminating personal opinion
(C) discussing cures for jet lag
(D) discussing a specific country
(E) none of the above

DIRECTIONS: Revise each of the sentences below according to the directions that follow it. Some directions require you to rephrase only part of the original sentence; others require you to recast the entire sentence. You may need to omit or add certain words in constructing an acceptable revision, but you should keep the meaning of your revised sentence as close to the meaning of the original sentence as the directions permit. Your new sentence should follow the conventions of standard written English and should be clear and concise.

Look through answer choices A-E under each question for the exact word or phrase that is included in your revised sentence. If you have thought of a revision that does not include any of the words or phrases listed, try to revise the sentence again so that it does include the wording in one of the answer choices.

39. Of all my friends none is more loyal and loving than Sean.

Substitute <u>Sean is</u> for <u>none is</u>.

(A) none but more loyal
(B) more loyal
(C) as loyal
(D) the most loyal
(E) the most loyalest

40. In the 1800's, many of a woman's duties were physically demanding; in addition, her status was much lower than it is today.

Put <u>when</u> before <u>many</u>.

(A) and her status was
(B) her status having been
(C) her status was
(D) her status being
(E) so her status was

41. Leaders in the movie industry predict that, because of the growing number of VCR owners, filmmakers will soon be inspired to produce films exclusively for home viewing.

Change <u>that, because</u> to <u>that the growing</u>.

(A) owners, and they have inspired
(B) owners had inspired
(C) owners, which have inspired
(D) owners, inspiring
(E) owners will inspire filmmakers

42. Before the book was published, the life and work of the artist were unknown to most people.

Change <u>were unknown</u> to <u>knew</u>.

(A) some
(B) everyone
(C) few
(D) someone
(E) anyone

43. The cello player carried his instrument down the street, and he stopped and played each time there was a halt in the parade.

Begin with Carrying his instrument.

(A) the cello player stopped and played
(B) and the cello player played it
(C) the cello player stopping and playing
(D) stopped and played the player of the cello
(E) the cello player stopped to be playing it

44. The prescription contained no harmful substances, merely a mild tranquilizer to soothe the actress's nerves.

Substitute which contained for contained.

(A) provided a mere tranquilizer
(B) merely tranquilized
(C) had merely tranquilized
(D) merely tranquilizes
(E) was a merest tranquilizer

45. Arriving at the airport early, she found no one waiting to meet her.

Change arriving to she arrived.

(A) and so she did find
(B) and found
(C) and has found
(D) and there she had found
(E) and then finding

DIRECTIONS: Each of the following passages consists of numbered sentences. Because the passages are part of longer writing samples, they do not necessarily constitute a complete discussion of the issues presented.

Read each passage carefully and answer the questions that follow it. The questions test your awareness of a writer's purpose and of characteristics of prose that are important to good writing.

Questions 46-50 are based on the following passage.

(1) The Elizabethan society was one in which speed was impossible and therefore not a matter for concern. (2) Distance was a stern reality. (3) A mile was not something that could be covered in a few minutes or seconds; it was a formidable length of land or water. (4) Thus England was a very big place to any traveler. (5) Most of its inhabitants never ventured far from the village in which they were born. (6) A person could move only as fast as the fastest horse. (7) Perhaps life in this period, with its slower pace, was happier and healthier than our own. (8) As a frequent victim of jet lag, I am inclined to believe that it definitely was.

46. Which of the following best describes the relationship of sentence 1 to the rest of the paragraph?

(A) It presents the idea that the rest of the paragraph goes on to develop.
(B) It demonstrates the writer's authority on the subject.
(C) It presents an idea that is refuted in the rest of the paragraph.
(D) It tells what method will be used to organize the paragraph.
(E) It directly compares Elizabethan society to our own.

47. In sentence 7, what is the effect of the phrase "than our own"?

(A) It restates the main idea.
(B) It draws a comparison between Elizabethan and modern society.
(C) It illustrates the superiority of modern travel.
(D) It gives another example of lack of speed in Elizabethan times.
(E) It emphasizes the similarities between Elizabethan society and modern society.

48. What should be done with sentence 2?

(A) "In any event" should be added at the beginning of the sentence.
(B) The verb was should be changed to is.
(C) It should be placed after sentence 5.
(D) It should be omitted.
(E) It should be left as it is.

49. What is the purpose of sentence 3?

(A) It restates the topic sentence.
(B) It makes the specific idea in sentence 2 more general.
(C) It shows a cause/effect relationship.
(D) It gives a specific example to enhance the generalization in sentence 2.
(E) It provides evidence to contradict sentence 1.

50. The purpose of the paragraph is primarily to

    (A) Give travelers hints about vacationing in England.
    (B) Show how superior our world is to that of the Elizabethans.
    (C) Present a detailed comparison of methods of travel then and now.
    (D) Point out, somewhat lovingly, the slower pace of life in Elizabethan times.
    (E) Complain about jet lag.

SHORT SAMPLE: EXPLANATORY ANSWERS
SECTION I

1. (B) The verb <u>is</u> needed to agree with the singular subject <u>dog</u>. <u>As well as five cats</u> is not part of the subject.

2. (E) No error.

3. (D) <u>Fewer</u> should be used to refer to a number of things. <u>Less</u> is used for a single quantity. (Fewer smokers..less smoke)

4. (D) Items in a series must be grammatically parallel. <u>Joining the army</u> would be a better phrase.

5. (B) The singular pronoun <u>he</u> is needed to refer to the singular antecedent <u>person</u>. The verb <u>are</u> should also be the singular <u>is</u>.

6. (D) In order to keep the tense of the sentence consistent the present verb <u>comes</u> is needed.

7. (A) This is an unnecessary shift from active to passive voice.

8. (B) The subjunctive <u>were</u> is needed in the <u>if</u> clause. (Condition expressed contrary to fact)

9. (E) No error.

10. (A) The case of the pronoun is incorrect. The objective <u>me</u> is needed after the preposition <u>between</u>.

11. (C) In the original sentence, the conjunction <u>and</u> does not establish the proper relationship between the two parts of the sentence. Choice (B) is incorrect because it is not generally good to begin a sentence with a coordinating conjunction. In (D) <u>since</u> causes the same problem as <u>and</u> does in (A). (E) is awkward and destroys the parallelism of the sentence. The best choice is (C). Notice that <u>however</u> is preceded by a semicolon and not by a comma.

12. (D) Answer (D) maintains the simplicity and parallelism of the first part of the sentence. (A) The pronoun <u>they</u> has no antecedent. The same is true in (E). (B) and (C) produce awkward sentences. (C) also would be incorrect in tense.

13. (B) Choice (B) transforms the original to natural subject-verb order and corrects the error in agreement. (A) and (D) have the incorrect verb was. Birds is a plural noun and needs a plural verb such as were. (C) does not flow smoothly; the word arrangement is awkward. (E) changes the original to a question and is also awkward.

14. (A) Answer (A) is smooth and clear. (B), (D), and (E) use the passive voice unnecessarily and ineffectively. (C) They is unnecessary in this revision.

15. (D) Answer (D) maintains the parallel structure necessary in not only... but constructions. None of the other choices does this. In addition, (A) and (B) are not idiomatic.

16. (B) Answer (A) is a run-on. (C) is passive, (D) is ambiguous and awkward. (E) has a misplaced modifier.

17. (C) All other choices would be inconsistent in pronoun person. The second part of the original contains the pronoun you. In choice (C) the subject is you understood.

18. (A) (B) is a run-on. (C) changes the meaning. (D) the part before the semicolon is a fragment. (E) The tense is incorrect.

19. (B) Parallel grammatical elements are needed in a series. Enjoy to is not idiomatic.

20. (E) Choice (E) is the clearest, simplest revision. (A) is wordy and ambiguous. (B) changes the meaning. (C) The ; makes the first part a fragment. (D) Reason being because is ungrammatical.

21. (C) Many of these animals had been abandoned, but some were lost pets whose owners could not be found.

22. (E) To help reunite owners with their lost cats, the city council approved an ordinance requiring cat owners to have an identifying microchip placed under the skin between the shoulder blades of their cats.

23. (A) It costs only about $5 and lasts the life of the cat. The verb must be changed to the present tense to maintain consistency.

24. (C) The author does all the things listed except criticize those whose opinions differ from his.

25. (B)   What are needed to end this tragedy are laws <u>that will not only curb breeding but will also facilitate</u> the identification of lost animals.

26. (A)   <u>An example of this law has already been passed in California.</u> This sentence best serves as an introduction to paragraph 2 as well as a transition from paragraph 1.

27. (D)   <u>Furthermore,</u> it costs only about $5 and lasts the life of the cat. The addition of an appropriate transition word and the tense change in question 23 make this a much more effective sentence.

SECTION II

28. (B)   The case of the pronoun is incorrect. The subjective <u>she</u> should be used as the subject of the verb <u>accepted</u>.

29. (E)   No error.

30. (A)   The verb <u>are</u> is needed to agree with the subject <u>problems</u>.

31. (A)   The verb should be <u>lying</u> (meaning <u>resting</u>).

32. (A)   <u>Would have</u> should not be used in a clause that begins with <u>if</u>. The sentence should begin <u>If we had known</u>.

33. (D)   The verb should be the present tense <u>loves</u> to maintain tense consistency in the sentence. (<u>Seems</u> is present tense.)

34. (C)   <u>However,</u> if you do a little preparation and keep your cool, it can be one of the most exciting, rewarding experiences you'll ever have.

35. (D)   This sentence includes all of the information, maintains parallelism and tense consistency, and eliminates general pronoun reference.

36. (A)   <u>When you arrive at your destination,</u> make your first stop the city's visitor center.

37. (A)   The sentence is clearest and smoothest <u>as it is now</u>.

38. (E)   <u>None of the suggestions</u> given would improve the paragraph.

39. (D)   Of all my friends, Sean is <u>the most loyal</u> and loving.

40. (C)   In the 1800's, when many of a woman's duties were physically demanding, <u>her status was</u> much lower than it is today.

41. (E) Leaders in the movie industry predict that the growing number of VCR <u>owners will inspire filmmakers</u> to produce films exclusively for home viewing.

42. (C) Before the book was published, <u>few</u> knew the life and work of the artist.

43. (A) Carrying his instrument down the street, <u>the cello player stopped and played</u> each time there was a halt in the parade.

44. (B) The prescription which contained no harmful substances <u>merely tranquilized</u> the actress's nerves.

45. (B) She arrived at the airport early <u>and found</u> no one waiting to meet her.

46. (A) This is the main idea the paragraph goes onto develop.

47. (B) This sentence draws a comparison between Elizabethan and modern society.

48. (E) The sentence is fine as it is.

49. (D) This is giving a specific example to further explain the generalization in sentence 2.

50. (D) The slower pace of life in Elizabethan times appears to be attractive to the writer.

After you have taken this short sample test, checked your answers, and reviewed your areas of weakness, you are ready to take the full length CLEP General Examination in English Composition which follows. When you take it, be sure to choose a quiet spot where you will not be disturbed, and time yourself accurately.

SAMPLE TEST

CLEP GENERAL EXAMINATION IN ENGLISH COMPOSITION
SECTION I
(OF BOTH TEST VERSIONS)

Time: 45 minutes   55 questions

DIRECTIONS: The following sentences contain problems in grammar, usage, diction (choice of words) and idiom. Some sentences are correct. No sentence contains more than one error. You will find that the error, if there is one, is underlined and lettered. Assume that elements of the sentence that are not underlined are correct and cannot be changed. In choosing answers, follow the requirements of standard written English.

If there is an error, select the <u>one underlined part</u> that must be changed to make the sentence correct and blacken the corresponding space on your answer sheet.

If there is no error, select answer (E).

1. <u>Ancient people found</u> <u>that when</u> you add tin to copper you make an alloy
        A   B
    that is harder and <u>more durable</u> than <u>bronze</u>. <u>No error</u>
                            C   D   E

2. Aerobics and jogging <u>are both</u> valuable physical activities; <u>if done</u>
                          A   B
    incorrectly, however, <u>it</u> <u>can cause</u> serious damage. <u>No error</u>
                          C   D   E

3. If we who <u>have</u> few responsibilities cannot complete the course, we
              A
    <u>cannot expect</u> that others <u>who have many problems</u> <u>to complete</u> it either.
        B   C   D
    <u>No error</u>
        E

111

4. Ruth <u>felt</u> <u>badly</u> <u>that her house</u> <u>would not be completed</u> in time for the
        A   B   C   D

   party. <u>No error</u>
          E

5. That loud argument <u>between Father and me</u> was <u>so annoying</u> that it
                                     A   B

   resulted in our <u>neighbors</u> calling the police <u>to complain</u>. <u>No error</u>
                    C   D   E

6. The exhibit <u>was opened</u> <u>by hundreds</u> of performers <u>dancing</u> around the
                  A   B   C

   platform <u>in beautiful costumes</u>. <u>No error</u>
                  D   E

7. The collar <u>that he wore</u> to the show was far <u>more expensive</u> and beautiful
                   A   B

   <u>than</u> <u>the other dogs</u>. <u>No error</u>
    C   D   E

8. If he had <u>laid</u> <u>quietly</u> in his place as he <u>had been trained</u> to do, he
             A   B   C

   <u>would have been</u> voted "Best in Show." <u>No error</u>
        D   E

9. Disclosure <u>by two newspapers</u> that the candidate <u>has received</u> <u>most of</u>
                 A   B   C

   his contributions from developers <u>have shocked</u> local voters. <u>No error</u>
                                    D   E

10. To avoid the traffic, <u>our plans</u> were that we <u>would leave</u> before sunrise
                         A   B

    and <u>arrive</u> at our destination <u>before rush hour</u>. <u>No error</u>
         C   D   E

11. Some of my <u>most romantic</u> and memorable journeys <u>have been</u> by train:
                 A   B

    from Leningrad to Moscow, from Paris to Istanbul, <u>through the Swiss</u>
                                                         C

    Alps, and <u>Japan's superspeed bullet train</u>. <u>No error</u>
     C   D   E

12   The campaign has been <u>one of political extremes</u> with neither candidate
                            A

      <u>making any effort</u> to moderate <u>their</u> extreme position <u>on the issues</u>.
             B   C   D
      <u>No error</u>
          E

13.   Wilson <u>changed</u> his mind <u>as a result</u> of the German <u>attitude of ignoring</u>
                   A   B   C

      their promise of not blowing up passenger ships and <u>they began</u> killing
                                                               D

      more Americans. <u>No error</u>
                          E

14.   When he <u>left</u>, I realized that <u>I forgot</u> <u>to give</u> him the copy of the book he
                  A   B   C

      <u>had requested</u>. <u>No error</u>
            D   E

15.   He is a <u>faster</u> skater than <u>me</u>; <u>therefore</u>, I do not enjoy racing <u>against</u>
                  A   B   C   D

      <u>him</u>. <u>No error</u>
          D   E

16.   <u>Irregardless</u> of what <u>you think</u>, I <u>am going</u> <u>to spend</u> my vacation in
            A   B   C   D
      Europe this summer. <u>No error</u>
                              E

17.   <u>When we look</u> in the dust of two million years ago <u>and find</u> fossils of the
            A   B

      creature <u>who was to become man</u>, we are struck by the tremendous
                        C

      <u>differences between</u> his skull and ours. <u>No error</u>
              D   E

DIRECTIONS: In each of the following sentences, some part or all of the sentence is underlined. Below each sentence you will find five ways of phrasing the underlined part. Select the answer that produces the most effective sentence, one that is clear and exact, without awkwardness or ambiguity. In choosing answers, follow the requirements of standard written English. Choose the answer that best expresses the meaning of the original sentence.

Answer (A) is always the same as the underlined part. Choose answer (A) if you think the original sentence needs no revision.

18. Riding a horse <u>is in some ways like when you are driving a racing car</u>.

   (A) is in some ways like when you are driving a racing car.
   (B) in some ways is in the same class as when you drive a racing car.
   (C) is in some ways similar to when you are driving a racing car.
   (D) is like a drive in some ways in a racing car.
   (E) is like driving a racing car.

19. <u>Having misbehaved in the restaurant on Friday, the crew deserved the severe reprimand they received</u>.

   (A) Having misbehaved in the restaurant on Friday, the crew deserved the severe reprimand they received.
   (B) Having misbehaved in the restaurant on Friday, the reprimand was deserved by the crew.
   (C) The crew, reprimand have been deserved by them on Friday, misbehaved in the restaurant.
   (D) The severe reprimand they received for their misbehavior in the restaurant on Friday, the crew deserved.
   (E) The reprimand for having misbehaved in the restaurant on Friday was deserved and received by the crew.

20. Teachers often say that <u>they, not scientists, have</u> the answer to the improvement of life in the future.

   (A) they, not scientists, have
   (B) it is not scientists but that they have
   (C) it is not scientists but it is they who have
   (D) it is them, not scientists, who have
   (E) it is they, not scientists, who have had

21. Known to everyone in town, <u>friends were never lacking to my father</u>.

    (A) friends were never lacking to my father.
    (B) friends never lacked my father.
    (C) my father had many friends.
    (D) many friends were had by my father.
    (E) my father never lacked no friends.

22. <u>No sooner had she arrived at the party and the band began to play</u>, and everyone began to dance.

    (A) No sooner had she arrived at the party and the band began to play
    (B) No sooner had she arrived at the party but the band began to play
    (C) No sooner had she arrived at the party the band began to play
    (D) As soon as she arrived at the party, the band began to play
    (E) As soon as she arrived at the party, than the band began to play

23. <u>Although the dogs differed in breed and size; they</u> were all able to get along together in the kennel.

    (A) Although the dogs differed in breed and size; they
    (B) The dogs having differed in breed and size
    (C) The dogs, which differed in breed and size,
    (D) The dogs differed in breed and size, they
    (E) When the dogs differed in breed and size, they

24. The suburban student is getting a better education; <u>there are better teachers and better facilities for them</u>.

    (A) there are better teachers and better facilities for them.
    (B) he has better teachers and better facilities.
    (C) they have better teachers and better facilities.
    (D) because they have better teachers and facilities.
    (E) there's better teachers and facilities for him.

25. <u>If you saw the amount of pancakes he ate at breakfast this morning</u>, you would understand why his food bill is so high.

    (A) If you saw the amount of pancakes he ate at breakfast this morning
    (B) If you would see the amount of pancakes he consumed this morning
    (C) If you had seen the number of pancakes he consumed this morning
    (D) If you will see the number of pancakes he consumed this morning
    (E) When you see the amount of pancakes he had eaten at breakfast this morning

26. The girl is a model in the blue dress.

    (A) The girl is a model in the blue dress.
    (B) The girl wearing the blue dress is a model.
    (C) The girl is a model wearing a blue dress.
    (D) Wearing the blue dress, the girl is a model.
    (E) A model is the girl in the blue dress.

27. When the members of the team disagree, and when also, in addition, they are in the process of learning new plays, problems arise.

    (A) and when also, in addition, they are in the process
    (B) they are in the process
    (C) and when the members of the team are in process
    (D) at the same time they are in the process
    (E) and also when they are in the process

28. Since no one can explain this as well as he, he will attempt to teach the course.

    (A) as well as he, he
    (B) as well as him, no one but him
    (C) as well as he does, no one but he all alone
    (D) as well as he, no one but himself
    (E) in a manner as fine as he, no one but he and he alone

29. Mary Smith was born on Christmas, she was also elected Christmas Dance Princess.

    (A) was born on Christmas, she was also elected Christmas Dance
        Princess.
    (B) on Christmas was born and was also elected Christmas Dance
        Princess.
    (C) , who was born on Christmas, was elected Christmas Dance Princess.
    (D) since she was born on Christmas and was also elected Christmas
        Dance Princess
    (E) having been born on Christmas had therefore been elected Christmas
        Dance Princess.

30. Jane enjoyed flying because she always seemed to get stuck in the middle seat of the row.

    (A) because she always seemed to get stuck in the middle seat of the row.
    (B) if she always seemed to get stuck in the middle seat of the row.
    (C) although she always seemed to get stuck in the middle seat of the
        row.
    (D) she always seemed to get stuck in the middle seat of the row.
    (E) being that she always seemed to get stuck in the middle seat of the
        row.

31. I enjoy looking out an airplane window <u>to see the rain, the clouds, and how the cities are lighted</u>.

    (A) to see the rain, the clouds, and how the cities are lighted.
    (B) to see it raining, the clouds, and the lights.
    (C) to see the rain, how clouds make strange formations, and the lights.
    (D) to see raindrops, cloud formations, and glittering lights.
    (E) to see raindrops, cloud formations, and lights that glitter.

32. <u>Seated by the window, her make-up carefully applied Kay</u>.

    (A) Seated by the window, her make-up carefully applied Kay.
    (B) Seated by the window, Kay carefully applied her make-up.
    (C) Kay carefully applied her make-up seated by the window.
    (D) Seated by the window, the make-up was carefully applied by Kay.
    (E) Kay, having seated herself by the window, carefully applied her make-up.

33. <u>Each of the five boys always play their best</u> against tough opponents.

    (A) Each of the five boys always play their best
    (B) Each of the five boys always plays their best
    (C) Each of the five boys always plays his best
    (D) Each of the five boys always play his best
    (E) Each of the five boys always plays always his best

34. The functions of a guidance counselor are <u>advising students on courses, helping them with problems, and keeping them out of trouble</u>.

    (A) advising students on courses, helping them with problems, and keeping them out of trouble.
    (B) to be an advisor to students, helping them with problems and keep them out of trouble.
    (C) to advise students on courses, helping them with problems, and keeping them out of trouble.
    (D) advising students on courses, helping them, and to keep them out of trouble.
    (E) to advise students on courses, helped them with problems, and to keep them out of trouble.

35. After Michael <u>would catch the long pass, he races</u> to the ten-yard line.

    (A) would catch the long pass, he races
    (B) would have caught the long pass, he would have raced
    (C) has caught the long pass, he raced
    (D) catches the long pass, he will race
    (E) will have caught the long pass, he raced

DIRECTIONS: Each of the following selections is an early draft of a student essay in which the sentences have been numbered for easy reference. Some parts of the selections need to be changed.

Read each selection and then answer the questions that follow. Some questions are about particular sentences or parts of sentences and ask you to improve sentence structure and diction (word choice). In making these decisions, follow the conventions of standard written English. Other questions refer to the entire essay or parts of the essay and ask you to consider organization, development, and effectiveness of language in relation to purpose and audience. After you choose each answer, fill in the corresponding oval on your answer sheet.

Questions 36-41 are based on the following early draft of a student essay:

(1) Doctors say Americans should cut down on fat. (2) Eating too much can lead to health problems, like heart disease. (3) One way to cut down is to give up ice cream forever and eat frozen yogurt. (4) Frozen yogurt is the fastest growing new food of the decade.

(5) First, compare the nutritional value of each food. (6) A serving of premium ice cream can have as much as 330 calories and 20 grams of fat. (7) Regular frozen yogurt has 150 calories and 3 grams of fat. (8) Nonfat frozen yogurt has only 80 calories and 0 grams of fat. (9) Clearly, the savings in calories and fat were worth at least a taste test. (10) But what about the taste? (11) Does whipping air and sugar into icy sour milk tempt you? (12) Actually, it's quite good. (13) The best is smooth, creamy, and sweet with a gentle yogurt tang.

(14) So why not give it a try? (15) All you've got to lose is all those calories and all that fat!

36. In the context of the first paragraph, which of the following is the best version of sentence 2 (reproduced below)?

Eating too much can lead to health problems, like heart disease.

(A) (As it is now)
(B) Eating too much will lead
(C) Eating too much of it can lead
(D) Too much eating of it can lead
(E) Much eating of it will lead

37. Which of the following sentences, if added after sentence 4, would **best** link the first paragraph with the rest of the essay?

(A) There are several reasons that this switch is a good idea.
(B) Have you ever tasted it?
(C) Research shows why this is a good idea.
(D) If you haven't tried it, now's the time.
(E) Ice cream won't be that hard to give up.

38. Which of the following is the best way to revise the underlined portions of sentences 3 and 4 (reproduced below) so that the two sentences are combined into one?

One way to cut down is to give up ice cream forever, and eat <u>frozen yogurt. Frozen yogurt is the fastest growing new food of the decade.</u>

(A) frozen yogurt, the fastest growing new food of the decade.
(B) frozen yogurt, which has been the fastest growing new food of the decade.
(C) frozen yogurt; the fastest growing new food of the decade.
(D) frozen yogurt, and it is the fastest growing new food of the decade.
(E) frozen yogurt, therefore, the fastest growing new food of the decade.

39. Which of the following is the best way to revise the underlined portions of sentences 7 and 8 (reproduced below) so that the two sentences are combined into one?

Regular frozen yogurt has 150 calories and 8 grams of fat. <u>Nonfat frozen yogurt has</u> only 80 calories and 0 grams of fat.

(A) , but nonfat frozen yogurt has
(B) although nonfat frozen yogurt has
(C) in addition, nonfat frozen yogurt had
(D) ; however, nonfat frozen yogurt has
(E) while nonfat frozen yogurt has

40. Which is the best version of the underlined portion of sentence 9 (reproduced below)?

Clearly, the savings in calories and fat <u>were worth</u> at least a taste test.

(A) (as it is now)
(B) had been worth
(C) are worth
(D) will be worth
(E) will have been worth

119

41. All of the following strategies are used by the writer of the passage **EXCEPT**

(A) developing the idea stated in sentence 3
(B) using reasons to support a generalization
(C) presenting factual information to support a reason
(D) telling a story
(E) suggesting a course of action

Questions 42-48 are based on the following early draft of a student essay.

(1) As soon as I realized that it wasn't a dream, two thoughts occurred to me almost simultaneously. (2) One, this is the big one, the 8.0 earthquake that scientists have been predicting for years. (3) Two, we're all going to die! (4) Fortunately, I was wrong on both counts. (5) January 17, 1994 will be etched in my mind as the day that forever changed my outlook on disaster preparedness and survival skills.

(6) I knew the drill for an earthquake: duck, cover and hold until the shaking stops. (7) I'd practiced it many times in my years of living in Los Angeles on 3.5 tremblors. (8) But no one had ever told me what to do during a violent 6.8 in total darkness at 4:30 in the morning. (9) I was thrown so violently I couldn't even get out of bed. (10) The fact that I managed to duck the furniture that had fallen on top of me was sheer luck. (11) Neither had anyone told me how to get safely out of a room where every piece of large furniture was smashed, splintered, and blocking exits. (12) Nor did anyone explain how to get the emergency supplies stored, according to directions, in the garage behind a door that was jammed and would not open.

(13) Time has passed, and the earth is, for the moment, still. (14) And, I've learned that there is no real way to prepare for a totally unpredictable disaster like an earthquake. (15) The best you can do is react, cope, and use whatever natural survival instincts you possess.

42. Which of the following is the best way to revise and combine sentences 4 and 5 (reproduced below)?

Fortunately, I was wrong on both <u>counts. January</u> 17, 1994 will be etched in my mind as the day that forever changed my outlook on disaster preparedness and survival skills.

(A) counts, but January
(B) counts, and January
(C) counts, so January
(D) counts; January
(E) counts since January

43. Which of the following is the best way to revise the underlined portion of sentence 7 (reproduced below)?

I'd practiced it many times <u>in my years of living in Los Angeles on 3.5 tremblors.</u>

(A) in my years of living on 3.5 tremblors in Los Angeles
(B) having lived in Los Angeles many years on 3.5 tremblors
(C) during 3.5 tremblors in my years of living in Los Angeles
(D) in Los Angeles while living on 3.5 tremblors
(E) in my years of living in Los Angeles during 3.5 tremblors

44. Which of the following is the best way to revise the underlined portions of sentences 8 and 9 (reproduced below) so that the two sentences are combined into one?

But no one had ever told me what to do during a violent 6.8 in total darkness at 4:30 in the <u>morning. I was thrown</u> so violently I couldn't even get out of bed.

(A) morning, and I was thrown
(B) morning, while being thrown
(C) morning, having been thrown
(D) morning, as if being thrown
(E) morning, to have been thrown

45. Which of the following would best replace "And" at the beginning of sentence 14?

(A) However
(B) Because
(C) Then
(D) While
(E) Furthermore

46. In the context of paragraph 3, which of the following is the best version of the underlined portion of sentence 15 (reproduced below)?

The best you can do is react, cope, and <u>use whatever natural survival instincts</u> you possess.

(A) (As it is now)
(B) using whatever natural survival skills
(C) having used whatever natural survival instincts
(D) whatever natural survival instincts are used
(E) do use natural instincts to survive

47. All of the following strategies are used by the writer of the passage **EXCEPT**

(A) selecting specific examples
(B) telling a story
(C) refuting a commonly held idea
(D) describing an emotional reaction
(E) providing statistical support for an argument

48. The writer of the passage could best improve sentence 7 by

(A) discussing other natural disasters
(B) acknowledging drawbacks to previous suggestions
(C) elaborating on personal opinion
(D) discussing the scientific principle of the Richter Scale
(E) describing or explaining "3.5"

Questions 49-55 are based on the following early draft of a student essay.

(1) People who love to read, read mysteries. (2) So do people who don't read much at all. (3) Teachers, cab drivers, teenagers, and grandmothers love mysteries.

(4) One reason might be that they help people feel the world is not out of control. (5) That unlike in life, the bad guys usually get caught and good people make a difference. (6) Another reason is that they're lots of fun to figure out. (7) It's a challenge to figure out "whodunit;" before the author reveals the culprit in the last chapter. (8) There's the suspense. (9) Mysteries move along very quickly. (10) You get to satisfy your urge to know what will happen next as long as you keep turning the pages.

49. Which of the following sentences, if added after sentence 3, would best link the first paragraph with the rest of the essay?

(A) Why does almost everyone love a mystery?
(B) Students love mysteries.
(C) Mysteries are made into movies.
(D) Mystery writers must make a lot of money.
(E) Who doesn't love a mystery?

50. Which of the following would best replace "they" in sentence 4?

(A) it
(B) them
(C) mysteries
(D) stories
(E) authors

51. Which of the following is the best way to revise the underlined portion of sentence 5 (reproduced below)?

That unlike in life, the bad guys usually get caught and good people make a difference.
(A) (As it is now)
(B) Unlike in real life,
(C) Not like it is in real life,
(D) Not like real life is,
(E) Like real life is not,

123

52. In the context of the second paragraph, which of the following should be placed at the beginning of sentence 8?

   (A) And,
   (B) However,
   (C) Finally,
   (D) Thus,
   (E) Therefore,

53. What is the best way to revise the underlined portion of sentence 7 (reproduced below)?

   It's a challenge to figure out "whodunit;" before the author reveals the culprit in the last chapter.

   (A) (As it is now)
   (B) "whodunit." Before
   (C) "whodunit" before
   (D) "whodunit" and before
   (E) "whodunit" while before

54. In the context of the second paragraph, which of the following is the best way to revise sentence 10 (reproduced below)?

   You get to satisfy your urge to know what will happen next as long as you keep turning the pages.

   (A) (As it is now)
   (B) We get to satisfy our urge to know what will happen next as long as we keep turning the pages.
   (C) They get to satisfy their urge to know what will happen next as long as they keep turning the pages.
   (D) The reader gets to satisfy his urge to know what will happen next as long as he keeps turning the pages.
   (E) All people get to satisfy their urge to know what will happen next as long as all keep turning the pages.

55. All of the following strategies are used by the author of the passage **EXCEPT**

   (A) supporting a generalization with reasons
   (B) giving specific examples to explain the reasons
   (C) presenting an opinion
   (D) telling a story
   (E) using transitional words to connect the reasons

SECTION II
(OF THE ALL MULTIPLE CHOICE TEST VERSION)

Time: 45 minutes   45 Questions

DIRECTIONS: The following sentences contain problems in grammar, usage, diction (choice of words), and idiom. Some sentences are correct. No sentence contains more than one error. You will find that the error, if there is one, is underlined and lettered. Assume that elements of the sentence that are not underlined are correct and cannot be changed. In choosing answers, follow the requirements of standard written English.

If there is an error, select the <u>one underlined part</u> that must be changed to make the sentence correct and blacken the corresponding space on your answer sheet.

If there is no error, select answer (E).

1.   <u>After much</u> consideration and debate, he decided <u>to do</u> the project <u>like</u>
      　　A   B   C
      you <u>suggested</u>. <u>No error</u>
      　　　　D　　　　　　E

2.   <u>In "A Christmas Carol" it</u> <u>tells about</u> the old <u>miser Scrooge</u> and the spirits
      　　　　　A　　　　　　　　B　　　　　　　　　C
      <u>who came to reform</u> him. <u>No error</u>
      　　　　D　　　　　　　　　　E

3.   A comma <u>does not indicate</u> a full stop, as a period <u>is doing</u>, but
      　　　　　　A　　　　　　　　　　　　　　　　　　B
      <u>divides the sentence</u> into readable parts <u>by indicating</u> pauses. <u>No error</u>
      　　　C　　　　　　　　　　　　　　　　D　　　　　　　　E

4.   <u>Us kids</u> <u>are forming</u> our own band and <u>will perform</u> next <u>summer</u> in the
      　A　　　B　　　　　　　　　　　　　C　　　　　D
      park. <u>No error</u>
      　　　　E

5.   <u>Well, Harry,</u> <u>you're</u> lack of knowledge of this unusual subject <u>is not</u> at
      　　A　　　　　B　　　　　　　　　　　　　　　　　　　　C
      <u>all uncommon</u>. <u>No error</u>
      　　D　　　　　　E

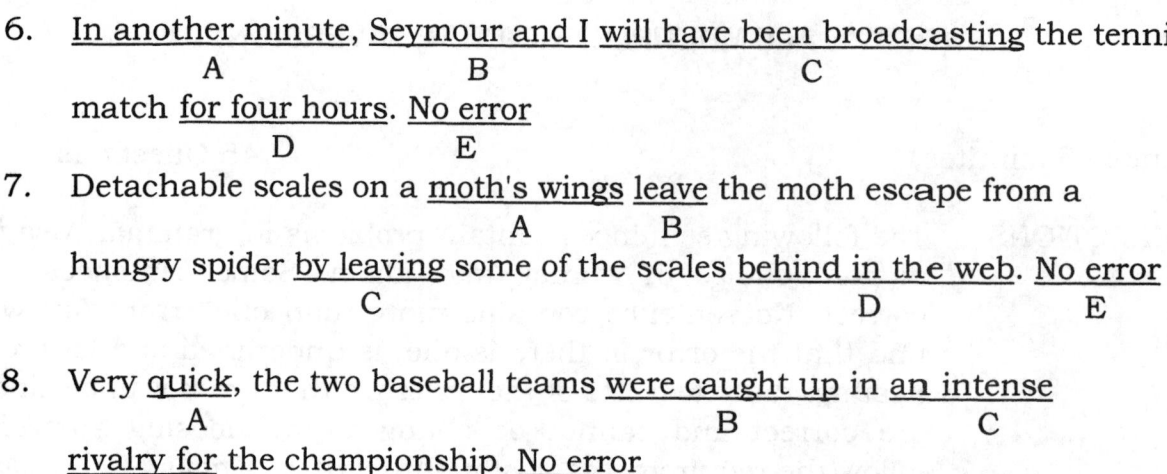

6. <u>In another minute,</u> <u>Seymour and I</u> <u>will have been broadcasting</u> the tennis
          A   B   C
    match <u>for four hours.</u> <u>No error</u>
          D   E

7. Detachable scales on a <u>moth's wings</u> <u>leave</u> the moth escape from a
                             A   B
    hungry spider <u>by leaving</u> some of the scales <u>behind in the web.</u> <u>No error</u>
                  C   D   E

8. Very <u>quick,</u> the two baseball teams <u>were caught up</u> in <u>an intense</u>
         A   B   C
    <u>rivalry for</u> the championship. <u>No error</u>
    D   E

9. The plant-eating dinosaurs <u>began</u> to die out <u>more sooner</u> <u>than</u> the
                                A   B   C
    <u>meat-eaters did.</u> <u>No error</u>
    D   E

10. <u>We girls</u> <u>couldn't hardly</u> finish all the food that <u>had been served</u> <u>to us</u> in
    A   B   C   D
    the restaurant. <u>No error</u>
                    E

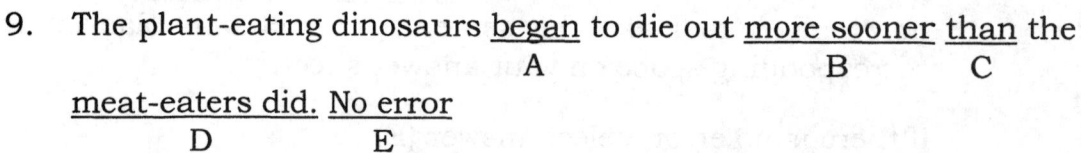

DIRECTIONS: Revise each of the sentences below according to the directions that follow it. Some directions require you to rephrase only part of the original sentence; others require you to recast the entire sentence. You may need to omit or add certain words in constructing an acceptable revision, but you should <u>keep the meaning of your revised sentence as close to the meaning of the original sentence as the directions permit</u>. Your new sentence should follow the conventions of standard written English and should be clear and concise.

Look through answer choices A-E under each question for the exact word or phrase that is included in your revised sentence. If you have thought of a revision that does not include any of the words or phrases listed, try to revise the sentence again so that it does include the wording in one of the answer choices.

11. The citizens were mistaken in their belief that giving out candy would discourage vandalism on Halloween.

    Begin with <u>Believing</u>.

    (A) was a mistake on the part of
    (B) was mistaken by
    (C) had proven to be a mistaken attempt by
    (D) was a mistake by
    (E) proved to be a mistake by

12. An old woman was frightened and chased yesterday afternoon near her home by three teenage boys.

    Begin with <u>Three teenage boys</u>.

    (A) frightened and began a chase
    (B) frightened and chasing
    (C) were frightened and chased
    (D) did frighten and chase
    (E) frightened and chased

13. In the past century, a different perspective on art has developed through a work of Picasso and others.

    Begin with <u>Picasso</u>.

    (A) and others have
    (B) with others will have
    (C) with others have
    (D) along with others have
    (E) has through the help of others

14. Don's search took him to Philadelphia, where he found Rosemary waiting to meet him.

    Begin with <u>Waiting to meet him</u>.

    (A) Rosemary had been discovered
    (B) Rosemary was found
    (C) Don found
    (D) Don discovered
    (E) Rosemary found

127

15. After selling millions of children's books, the author decided to begin writing literature for adults.

    Substitute <u>who had sold</u> for <u>After selling</u>.

    (A) books; decided
    (B) books, decided
    (C) books. He
    (D) books, however
    (E) books; however,

16. Of all his characters, Dickens never has created anyone more evil and unsympathetic than Bill Sikes.

    Substitute <u>created</u> for <u>never has created</u>.

    (A) hardly no one
    (B) none
    (C) not hardly any
    (D) hardly none
    (E) not a single one

17. The climate of Southern California is typically warm and dry.

    Begin with <u>Warm and dry weather</u>.

    (A) in the manner of
    (B) in accordance with
    (C) typically
    (D) typical of
    (E) in addition to

18. The superstar was responsible for selling more tickets to the movies than anyone else; consequently, he received millions of dollars per picture.

    Begin with <u>Since</u>.

    (A) else, he
    (B) else; he
    (C) else, consequently
    (D) else; consequently
    (E) else, therefore

19. Given her strong drive for success and workaholic tendencies, it is fortunate that we were able to have lunch with her.

    Begin with <u>That we were able</u>.

    (A) we are fortunate in having
    (B) is a fortunate thing considering
    (C) should be fortunate
    (D) will always be fortunate
    (E) we are in good fortune

20. The exhibit was attended by some very prominent citizens of our community.

    Begin with <u>Some very prominent citizens</u>.

    (A) were attended
    (B) had to attend
    (C) attended
    (D) showed up at
    (E) duly were asked to attend

21. The terrorists planted a bomb at the airport to publicize their grievances.

    Begin with <u>Because they</u>.

    (A) grieved
    (B) were grieving
    (C) wanted
    (D) were wanting
    (E) were wanted

22. To write well a person must know how to think, organize, evaluate and revise.

    Change <u>To write</u> to <u>Writing</u>.

    (A) requires a person to know
    (B) requiring a person to know
    (C) requires a person knowing
    (D) requires that a person must have known
    (E) must a person be required to know

DIRECTIONS: Each of the following selections is an early draft of a student essay in which the sentences have been numbered for easy reference. Some parts of the selections need to be changed.

Read each selection and then answer the questions that follow. Some questions are about particular sentences or parts of sentences and ask you to improve sentence structure and diction (word choice). In making these decisions, follow the conventions of standard written English. Other questions refer to the entire essay or parts of the essay and ask you to consider organization, development, and effectiveness of language in relation to purpose and audience. After you choose each answer, fill in the corresponding oval on your answer sheet.

Questions 23-27 are based on the following early draft of a letter to the editor of a local newspaper.

(1) "Not in my back yard!" is a familiar cry of protest against the construction of any undesirable facility close to home. (2) No one seems to want a prison, a traffic producing tourist attraction, or especially a toxic waste dump in his community. (3) As with most clichés, there is an element of truth in this one. (4) The point is, why take a chance?

(5) Then there's the possibility of ground water contamination. (6) No matter how carefully the pellets are buried. (7) How do we know they won't seep into the ground water? (8) Then there's the transport trucks. (9) If there is an accident on one of our busy highways, the canisters could be shattered, releasing lethal doses of radiation.

(10) The federal government should find a less populated site for the project. (11) I cannot comprehend how they could even consider putting it so close to a city of 100,000. (12) Why not put this issue on the ballot? (13) People should have the opportunity to vote to protect the health and safety of their homes and community.

23. Which of the following sentences, if added after sentence 4, would best link the first paragraph with the rest of the letter?

(A) Putting a repository for high level radioactive waste within ten miles of our community is sowing the seeds for a potential disaster.
(B) They shouldn't put a toxic waste dump within ten miles of our community.
(C) Having put a high level radioactive waste dump within ten miles of us will cause a disaster.
(D) How can anyone do this to our community?
(E) I don't want any of these things in my community either.

24. In the context of the second paragraph, which of the following words would best replace the word "Then" at the beginning of sentence 5?

(A) Now
(B) Therefore
(C) Finally
(D) Next
(E) First

25. Which of the following is the best way to revise and combine sentences 6 and 7 (reproduced below)?

No matter how carefully the pellets are buried. How do we know they won't seep into the ground water?

(A) After how carefully they are buried, how do we know pellets won't seep into the ground water?
(B) No matter how carefully the pellets are buried, how do we know they won't seep into the ground water?
(C) No matter how carefully the pellets are buried; how do we know they won't seep into the ground water?
(D) How do we know after being buried the pellets won't be seeping into the ground water?
(E) After being buried, we don't know if the pellets will be seeping into the ground water.

26. Which is the best version of the underlined portion of sentence 8 (reproduced below)?

Then <u>there's</u> the transport trucks.

(A) (as it is now)
(B) there is
(C) there are
(D) there could be
(E) there have been

27. All of the following strategies are used by the author of the letter **EXCEPT**

(A) expressing a personal opinion
(B) stating a cliché
(C) refuting the argument presented in sentence 3
(D) setting forth possible negative consequences
(E) suggesting a possible solution to the dispute

<u>Questions 28-32</u> are based on the following early draft of a newspaper feature article.

(1) Juggling 15 credits in college, a part-time job, and an internship, Joe College has added another task to his schedule: looking for a job in his field now that graduation is only a few months away. (2) It won't be easy!

(3) Many companies have been hurt by the recession. (4) They are not in a hurry to hire. (5) In addition, automation has replaced thousands of jobs. (6) Also, in the next ten years the number of jobs is expected to grow by only 1.5% a year according to the U.S. Department of Labor.

(7) So what should Joe do? (8) Hang in there! (9) Recruiters say that regardless of the employment outlook, there's a job out there if you are determined to find one. (10) Graduates of a four-year college stand the best chance to get a good job at good pay.

28. Which of the following sentences, if added after sentence 2, would best link the first paragraph with the rest of the article?

(A) Recruiters have a lot of problems too.
(B) It's a tough job market out there for everyone.
(C) Joe should follow these steps.
(D) What should he do?
(E) Maybe he'd better try to get into graduate school.

29. Which of the following is the best way to revise and combine sentences 3 and 4 (reproduced below)?

    Many companies have been hurt by the recession. They are not in a hurry to hire.

    (A) Having been hurt by the recession, they are not in a hurry to hire.
    (B) Many companies, having hurt themselves in the recession, are not in a hurry to hire.
    (C) Many companies, hurt by the recession, aren't in a hurry to hire.
    (D) Many companies have been hurt by the recession, but they are not in a hurry to hire.
    (E) The recession has hurt companies who are not hiring.

30. Which is the best version of the underlined portion of sentence 9 (reproduced below)?

    Recruiters say that regardless of the employment outlook, there's a job out there if you are determined to find one.

    (A) (as it is now)
    (B) if he is determined to find one
    (C) for people determined to find one
    (D) for those of you who are determined to find one
    (E) if you can find one

31. In the context of the third paragraph, which of the following would best be added at the beginning of sentence 10?

    (A) Furthermore
    (B) And
    (C) Therefore
    (D) Nevertheless
    (E) So

32. All of the following strategies are used by the author of the article **EXCEPT**

    (A) providing discouraging information
    (B) providing encouragement
    (C) citing statistics
    (D) presenting an opinion
    (E) discussing specific job hunting strategies

Each of the following passages consists of numbered sentences. Because the passages are part of longer writing samples, they do not necessarily constitute a complete discussion of the issues presented.

Read each passage carefully and answer the questions that follow it. The questions test your awareness of a writer's purpose and of characteristics of prose that are important to good writing.

Questions 33-38 are based on the following passage:

(1) Much is being written this year about the generation known as the "Baby Boomers." (2) The 76 million Americans born between 1946 and 1964 have reached mid-life; the first group is turning fifty next year. (3) Known at various times as the "Spock generation," the "Now generation," and the "Me generation," and referred to by demographers as "the pig in the python," they have been locked together in a crowded race their entire lives. (4) Because of their number, they have been forced to fight for places in college, jobs, and housing. (5) There are simply too many of them to maintain the lifestyle in which they had grown up. (6) The question remains as to what the second half of their lives will be like. (7) Providing pensions, health care, social security and other benefits, for a generation that promises to live longer than any before it, will be a great challenge for our country.

33. What is the purpose of sentence 1?

(A) It provides a general introduction to the topic.
(B) It presents the main idea of the paragraph.
(C) It defines the main term used in the paragraph.
(D) It forecasts the main term used in the paragraph.
(E) It presents a specific idea to be developed in a more general manner.

34. What is the function of sentence 2?

(A) It provides a general introduction to the paragraph.
(B) It contradicts the first sentence.
(C) It defines the term "Baby Boomers."
(D) It establishes the organization of the paragraph as a whole.
(E) It presents a solution to the problem presented in the paragraph.

35. The metaphor "pig in the python," in sentence 3 is used to show

    (A) that the Baby Boomers behave like pigs
    (B) that the Baby Boomers devour each other
    (C) that the Baby Boomers are reaching mid-life
    (D) that the Baby Boomers are a colorful group
    (E) that the Baby Boomers constitute a large bulge as they move through an otherwise even distribution of population

36. The main idea of this paragraph is

    (A) Baby Boomers will have unhappy lives as they grow older.
    (B) Baby Boomers will have it easier as they grow older.
    (C) the Baby Boomers will continue to present problems and challenges to the nation as they grow older.
    (D) Baby Boomers need a new name as the ones in the article are now out of date.
    (E) more needs to be written about the Baby Boomers.

37. If this paragraph were to be cut, the best place to begin paragraph 2 would be with

    (A) sentence 7
    (B) sentence 6
    (C) sentence 5
    (D) sentence 4
    (E) sentence 3

38. In sentence 3 what is the effect of the expression "at various times"?

    (A) It emphasizes the fact that the Baby Boomers are turning 50.
    (B) It reveals the writer's uncertainty about the names given to the Baby Boomers.
    (C) It emphasizes the crowdedness of the life of this generation.
    (D) It prepares the reader for the fact that different names have been used at different times to refer to the Baby Boomers.
    (E) It prepares the reader for an analysis of the various names given to the Baby Boomers.

Questions 39-45 are based on the following passage:

(1) The principle that the atom has constituent parts is the intellectual breakthrough with which modern physics begins. (2) The Greek name "atom" had implied that the particle was indivisible. (3) On the contrary, it was discovered that there were several particles contained within the atom: the proton, the neutron, and the electron. (4) The electron is important because each element is characterized by the number of these single electrically charged particles in its atom. (5) Thus the place in the table of elements that a particular element occupies is called its atomic number. (6) This number stands for the number of electrons in its atom.

39. Which of the following best describes the relationship of sentence 1 to the rest of the paragraph?

(A) It establishes the organization for the paragraph as a whole.
(B) It establishes the extreme importance of the principle upon which the remainder of the paragraph is based.
(C) It describes an idea that will be refuted in the rest of the paragraph.
(D) It introduces the procedure for classifying elements.
(E) It forces the reader to make an independent judgment about the material to follow.

40. Which best describes the function of sentence 2?

(A) It provides historical background on the discovery of the atom.
(B) It generalized the statement in sentence 1.
(C) It gives information on the origin of meaning of the word "atom."
(D) It paraphrases the information in sentence 1.
(E) It states the main idea of the paragraph.

41. Which best describes the purpose of sentence 3?

(A) It restates the information given in sentences 1 and 2.
(B) It demonstrates the writer's authority on the subject to be discussed.
(C) It contradicts the information given in sentence 2.
(D) It explains the importance of classification of elements.
(E) It analyzes the effect of a scientific discovery on society.

42. The organizing principle behind this paragraph is:

(A) moving from a general statement to a specific application.
(B) moving from a specific application to a general application.
(C) cause and effect.
(D) chronological development of a process.
(E) a spatial presentation of an argument.

43. In order to determine atomic number, this paragraph explains that the electron is the key. This idea is put forth in

(A) sentence 3
(B) sentence 5 and 6
(C) sentence 1
(D) sentences 1 and 2
(E) sentences 4, 5 and 6

44. Which treatment of sentence 5 is most needed?

(A) Leave it as it is.
(B) It should be placed after sentence 6.
(C) It should be omitted.
(D) "Thus" should be changed to "In addition."
(E) "That a particular element occupies" should be changed to "that is occupied by a particular element."

45. The purpose of this paragraph is primarily to

(A) tell the story of the discovery of the particles inside the atom.
(B) demonstrate the importance of protons, neutrons and electrons.
(C) propose a change in the organization of the table of elements.
(D) give the Greeks credit for their scientific genius.
(E) explain how elements are placed on the table of elements and point out the importance of the concept that the atom can be split.

SECTION II
(OF THE MULTIPLE CHOICE/ESSAY VERSION)

Time: 45 minutes

DIRECTIONS: You will have 45 minutes to plan and write an essay on the topic specified. Read the topic carefully. You are expected to spend a few moments considering the topic and organizing your thoughts before you begin writing. Do not write on a topic other than the one specified. An essay on a topic of your own choice is not acceptable.

The essay is intended to give you an opportunity to demonstrate your ability to write effectively. Take care to express your thoughts on the topic clearly and to make them of interest to the reader. Be specific, use supporting examples whenever appropriate. Remember that how well you write is much more important than how much you write.

SAMPLE TOPIC: For the past three decades the U. S. Space Program has been the subject of much debate. Some critics feel that the billions of dollars spent could be directed to more practical concerns such as feeding the world's hungry. Supporters of the program argue that space is a frontier that must be explored.

Should the United States continue to spend billions of dollars on the space program or should the money be directed to other areas? Be sure to support your opinion with reasons and examples.

SAMPLE TEST: EXPLANATORY ANSWERS
SECTION I

1. (E)   No error.

2. (C)   The pronoun <u>it</u> does not have a clear antecedent.

3. (D)   Faulty parallelism. It should read <u>will complete</u>.

4. (B)   The adjective <u>bad</u> is needed after the linking verb <u>feel</u>.

5. (C)   The possessive <u>neighbor's</u> is needed before the gerund <u>calling</u>.

6. (D)   Misplaced modifier. <u>In beautiful costumes</u> should follow <u>performers</u>, the word it describes.

7. (D)   Improper comparison. It should read <u>the other dog's collars</u>.

8. (A)   The past participle of the verb <u>lay</u> (to rest) is <u>lain</u>.

9. (E)   No error.

10. (A)   Dangling modifier. It should read <u>To avoid the traffic, we</u>.

11. (D)   Faulty parallelism. All other items in the series are expressed in prepositional phrases.

12. (C)   The singular pronoun <u>he</u> is needed to agree with the singular antecedent <u>neither candidate</u>.

13. (D)   Faulty parallelism. It should read <u>killing more Americans</u>.

14. (B)   Tense inconsistency. The past perfect <u>had forgotten</u> is needed since the action in B took place before the action in A.

15. (B)   It should read <u>He is a faster skater than I</u> (am).

16. (A)   Diction. The word <u>irregardless</u> is not standard English.

17. (E)   No error.

18. (E)   This choice maintains parallelism. The others are either wordy or awkward.

19. (A)   This is the only choice that has clear modification. All other choices are either awkward or unclear.

20. (A)   (B) and (D) ungrammatical. (C) is wordy. (E) unnecessarily changes the tense of the second verb.

21. (C)   (A) is awkward and wordy. (B) changes the meaning. (D) unnecessarily uses the passive. (E) is ungrammatical (double negative).

22. (D)   This is the only answer that maintains parallelism and retains the original meaning.

23. (C)   (A) is incorrectly punctuated. The ; should be a comma. (B) shifts tense unnecessarily. (D) creates a run-on sentence. (E) changes the meaning.

24. (B)   Student is singular and must be referred to by the singular pronoun he.

25. (C)   Number and not amount should be used with an item that can be counted, such as pancakes. The tense should not be future (will see) so choice (D) would be incorrect.

26. (B)   Choices (A) and (C) have misplaced modifier. (D) and (E) are awkward.

27. (D)   (A) is redundant. (B) changes the meaning. (C) and (E) are unnecessarily wordy.

28. (A)   (B) is incorrect because the pronoun he not him is needed as the subject of both clauses. (C) and (E) are too wordy. (D) himself is incorrect.

29. (C)   (A) creates a run-on. (B) and (E) are awkward and wordy. (D) creates a sentence fragment.

30. (C)   (A), (B), and (E) do not make sense when attached to part one of the sentence. (D) creates a run-on sentence.

31. (D)   This is the only choice that maintains parallel grammatical structure.

32. (B)   (A), (C), and (D) have dangling or misplaced modifiers. (E) is wordy.

33. (C)   Each needs the singular verb plays and the singular pronoun his. (E) is awkward.

34. (A) This is the only choice that maintains grammatical parallelism for all three items.

35. (D) This is the only choice that contains a correct, logical tense sequence.

36. (C) Eating too much of it can lead to health problems, like heart disease.

37. (A) There are several reasons that this switch is a good idea. This sentence tells what will follow in the next paragraph.

38. (A) One way to cut down is to give up ice cream and eat frozen yogurt, the fastest growing new food of the decade.

39. (E) Regular frozen yogurt has 150 calories and 3 grams of fat while nonfat frozen yogurt has only 80 calories and 0 grams of fat.

40. (C) Clearly, the savings in calories and fat are worth at least a taste test. Change is needed to maintain tense consistency in the essay.

41. (D) Telling a story to develop a point is not used in the passage.

42. (A) Fortunately, I was wrong on both counts, but January 17, 1994 will be etched in my mind as the day that forever changed my outlook on disaster preparedness and survival skills. The conjunction but best expresses the relationship between the ideas in the two sentences.

43. (C) I'd practiced many times during 3.5 tremblors in my years of living in Los Angeles. This choice corrects the misplaced phrase on 3.5 tremblors. In addition, during is a better preposition than on for this sentence.

44. (B) But no one had ever told me what to do during a violent 6.8 in total darkness at 4:30 in the morning, while being thrown so violently I couldn't even get out of bed.

45. (A) However, I've learned that there is no real way to prepare for a totally unpredictable disaster like an earthquake.

46. (A) The best you can do is react, cope, and use whatever natural survival instinct you possess. The best version for tense, smoothness, and parallelism is the sentence <u>as it is</u> in the essay.

47. (E) <u>No statistical support is provided.</u>

48. (E) <u>Describing or explaining "3.5"</u> would improve this sentence.

49. (A) <u>Why does almost everyone love a mystery?</u> This sentence states the question the author goes on to answer in the next paragraph.

50. (C) One reason might be that <u>mysteries</u> help us feel the world is not out of control. <u>Mysteries</u> helps tie the two paragraphs together and eliminates the vague pronoun <u>they</u>.

51. (B) <u>Unlike in real life</u>, the bad guys usually get caught and good people make a difference.

52. (C) <u>Finally</u>, there's the suspense.

53. (C) It's a challenge to figure out <u>"whodunnit" before</u> the author reveals the culprit in the last chapter.

54. (D) <u>The reader gets to satisfy his urge to know what will happen next as long as he keeps turning the pages.</u>

55. (D) The author <u>does not tell a story.</u>

SECTION II

1. (C) <u>As</u> not <u>like</u> introduces a clause.

2. (A) Unnecessary repetition. "<u>A Christmas Carol" tells about</u> is better.

3. (B) Faulty parallelism. <u>Is doing</u> should be <u>does</u>.

4. (A) The pronoun <u>us</u> cannot be used as the subject of a sentence. It should be replaced by the pronoun <u>we</u>.

5. (B) The contraction <u>you're</u> (you are) should be replaced by the pronoun <u>your</u>.

6. (E) No error.

7. (B) The verb <u>leave</u> (go away) should be replaced by the verb <u>let</u> (allow).

8. (A) The adjective <u>quick</u> is incorrect. It should be replaced by the adverb <u>quickly</u>.

9. (B) <u>More sooner</u> is a double comparison. It should be changed to <u>sooner</u>.

10. (B) <u>Couldn't hardly</u> is incorrect (double negative). It should be <u>could hardly</u>.

11. (A) Believing that giving out candy on Halloween would discourage vandalism <u>was a mistake on the part of</u> the citizens.

12. (E) Three teenage boys <u>frightened and chased</u> an old woman yesterday afternoon near her home.

13. (A) Picasso <u>and others have</u> developed a different perspective on art through their work.

14. (B) Waiting to meet him, <u>Rosemary was found</u> in Philadelphia by Don.

15. (B) The author, who had sold millions of children's <u>books, decided</u> to begin writing literature for adults.

16. (B) Of all his characters, Dickens created <u>none</u> more evil and sympathetic than Bill Sikes.

17. (D) Warm and dry weather is <u>typical of</u> the climate of Southern California.

18. (A) Since the superstar was responsible for selling more tickets to the movies than anyone <u>else, he</u> received millions of dollars per picture.

19. (B) That we were able to have lunch with her <u>is a fortunate thing considering</u> her strong drive for success and workaholic tendencies.

20. (C) Some very prominent citizens of our community <u>attended</u> the exhibit.

21. (C) Because they <u>wanted</u> to publicize their grievances, the terrorists planted a bomb at the airport.

22. (A) Writing well <u>requires a person to know</u> how to think, organize, evaluate, and revise.

23. (A)   <u>Putting a repository for high level radioactive waste within ten miles of our community is sowing the seeds for potential disaster.</u> This sentence states the main idea to be supported in the rest of the letter.

24. (E)   <u>First</u> there's the possibility of ground water contamination.

25. (B)   <u>No matter how carefully the pellets are buried, how do we know they won't seep into the ground water?</u> In the original letter, sentence 6 is a fragment and should be joined with sentence 7.

26. (C)   Then <u>there are</u> the transport trucks. This choice corrects the error in agreement of subject and verb and maintains tense consistency. The subject of the sentence <u>trucks</u> needs the plural verb <u>are</u>.

27. (C)   The author does <u>not refute the statement in sentence 3.</u> He goes on to support it.

28. (B)   <u>It's a tough job market out there for everyone.</u> This sentence best prepares the reader for the ideas to be developed in the article.

29. (C)   <u>Many companies, hurt by the recession, aren't in a hurry to hire.</u> This is the simplest, most direct, combination of the two sentences.

30. (C)   Recruiters say that regardless of the employment outlook, there's a job out there <u>for people determined to find one.</u> This choice avoids the use of the general <u>you</u> used in the original. <u>He</u> would also be incorrect in this sentence.

31. (A)   <u>Furthermore,</u> graduates of a four year college stand the best chance to get a good job at good pay.

32. (E)   The article <u>does not discuss specific job hunting strategies.</u>

33. (A)   The sentence provides a general introduction to the topic.

34. (C)   It defines Baby Boomers as the 76 million Americans born between 1946 and 1964.

35. (E)   The comparison shows how the Baby Boomers constitute a large bulge as they move through an otherwise even distribution of population. A python swallows its prey whole and the prey is a visible bulge as it moves into the snake.

36. (C) The main idea is that the Baby Boomers will continue to present problems to the nation as they grow older. These problems are due to their large numbers.

37. (B) The question of what the second half of their lives will be like (sentence 6) could be used to begin a new paragraph.

38. (D) It prepares the reader for different names used <u>at various times</u>.

39. (B) It states that the principle is the key to modern physics.

40. (C) It gives the origin of the word "atom".

41. (C) <u>On the contrary</u> indicates a contradiction of information preceding it.

42. (A) A paragraph begins with a generalization and moves to more specific information.

43. (E) It takes all three sentences to fully develop the concept.

44. (A) The sentence should <u>remain as it is.</u>

45. (E) The paragraph has a dual purpose although the explanation of classification of elements is the key idea.

Review Of Basic Grammar

Grammatical terms are a special kind of vocabulary. If you had difficulty understanding the rules of grammar presented in the main part of the text, review this section.

The following pages are designed to provide background for and a supplement to the rules presented in the body of the text. They will not repeat material already covered.

REVIEW OF BASIC TERMINOLOGY

Do you remember the eight basic parts of speech in English? Take this simple matching test to see.

PARTS OF SPEECH

DIRECTIONS: Match the part of speech with the correct definition and example.

1.____NOUN

2.____PRONOUN

3.____ADJECTIVE

4.____VERB

5.____ADVERB

6.____PREPOSITION

7.____CONJUNCTION

8.____INTERJECTION

A. action or state of being word: <u>run</u>, <u>is</u>

B. an exclamation: an unrelated word which expresses feeling: set off from the rest of a sentence by a comma or exclamation point: <u>Alas</u>! <u>Oh</u>!

C. name of a person, place, thing, or quality: <u>John</u>, <u>man</u>, <u>honesty</u>

D. word that describes or limits a noun or pronoun: tells <u>which</u>, <u>what kind of</u> or <u>how many</u>: <u>short</u>, <u>beautiful</u>, <u>honest</u>

E. word used in place of a noun: <u>I</u>, <u>you</u>, <u>who</u>

F. word used to join words or groups of words: <u>and</u>

G. word that modifies a verb, adjective, or adverb, tells <u>how</u>, <u>when</u>, <u>where</u>, <u>why</u>, <u>how often</u>: <u>carefully</u>, <u>now</u>, <u>quickly</u>

H. shows the relationship of a noun or pronoun to another word in the sentence: <u>to</u> the house <u>after</u> me

ANSWERS: 1. C, 2. E, 3. D, 4. A, 5. G, 6. H, 7. F, 8. B

The next few pages will review common grammatical problems associated with each part of speech. Before we do that, however, it is necessary to review the basic components of a sentence in English.

PYRAMID OF LANGUAGE

WORD
<u>(parts of speech)</u>

PHRASE
<u>(group of related words acting
together as one part of speech; not
containing both a subject and verb)</u>

CLAUSE
<u>(group of related words containing a subject and a verb)</u>

SENTENCE*
<u>(group of words containing a subject and a verb and
expressing a complete thought)</u>

PARAGRAPH
<u>(group of sentences organized around a central or main idea)</u>

* The basic grammatical unit we will be considering is the sentence.

PARTS OF A SENTENCE

VERB: a word that expresses action or helps to make a statement.

The key to a sentence is the verb. Always locate it first.

SUBJECT: a word or words naming person, place, thing, or idea about which something is being said.

To find the subject, ask the question <u>Who</u>? or <u>What</u>? before the verb.

In English, the normal pattern for the make-up of a sentence is SUBJECT-VERB-COMPLETER.

In a question, inverted order sentence, or sentence beginning with an adverb (<u>here</u>, <u>there</u>), change the word order so that subject is followed by the verb before you analyze the sentence.

EXAMPLE: On the shelf were the dishes.

The <u>dishes</u> <u>were</u> on the shelf.
      S   V

What book are you reading?

<u>You</u> <u>are reading</u> what book?
 S   V

Here is the book you ordered.

The <u>book</u> you ordered <u>is</u> here.
   S   V

COMPOUND SUBJECT/COMPOUND VERB: Two or more subjects or verbs connected by <u>and</u> or <u>or</u>.

EXAMPLE: <u>Milk and cookies</u> are on the table.
     C.S.

<u>Victory or defeat</u> comes at the end of every race.
    C.S.

The children <u>read and played</u> all afternoon.
        C.V.

DIRECT OBJECT: A noun or pronoun that answers the question <u>whom</u> or <u>what</u> after an action verb. It receives the action of the verb.

EXAMPLE: The teacher hit the <u>student</u>.
              D.O.

She hit <u>him</u>.
    D.O.

SUBJECT COMPLEMENT/PREDICATE NOMINATIVE: A noun or pronoun (or adjective) which follows a <u>be</u> or <u>linking verb</u> and renames or describes the subject. (Think of a <u>be</u> or <u>linking verb</u> as an = sign)

EXAMPLE: Mary is a <u>student</u>.
    S.C.

Mary is <u>intelligent</u>.
    S.C.

Mary became a <u>student</u>.
    S.C.

REVIEW OF CORRECT USAGE

(RELATED TO PARTS OF SPEECH)

A. NOUNS

A common noun labels any person, place, thing, or idea.

EXAMPLE: <u>dog</u>, <u>house</u>, <u>boy</u>

A proper noun labels a specific person, place, thing, or idea.

EXAMPLE: <u>Fido</u>, <u>White House</u>, <u>Frank</u>

Nouns are both plural and singular. The subject noun and the verb must **agree** in number.

EXAMPLE: <u>John</u> <u>is</u> the winner of the contest.

        S.   V.

    <u>The boys</u> <u>are</u> the winners of the contest.

        S.   V.

The possessive case is used to show ownership. The following rules are helpful in forming the possessive of a noun:

Singular nouns form the possessive by adding '<u>s</u>.

EXAMPLE: Mary's book

         a dog's collar

         the class's assignment

Plural nouns ending in <u>s</u> form the possessive by adding an apostrophe after the <u>s</u>'.

EXAMPLE: the dogs' bones

         the coaches' association

Plural nouns that do not end in <u>s</u> form the possessive by adding '<u>s</u>.

EXAMPLE: the women's dresses

         mice's cheese

B. PRONOUNS

Pronouns have three forms or cases:

NOMINATIVE	**OBJECTIVE**	**POSSESSIVE**
(used as subject or subject complement)	(used as an object of verb or of preposition)	(shows ownership)
		NOTE: possessive pronouns do not have apostrophes.
I	Me	My, Mine
You	You	You, Yours
He	Him	His
She	Her	Her, Hers
It	It	Its
We	Us	Our, Ours
They	Them	Their, Theirs
Who	Whom	Whose
Whoever	Whomever	Whosoever

Let us look at some applications of the above information.

SUBJECT = NOMINATIVE CASE

EXAMPLE: Mary and <u>he</u> are going.

HINT: In the case of a compound subject or object, say each separately with the verb.

Mary is going.

He (not <u>him</u>) is going.

OBJECT OF VERB = OBJECTIVE CASE

EXAMPLE: Father expects Fred and <u>me</u> for dinner.

Father expects Fred.

Father expects me. (not <u>I</u>)

SUBJECT OF UNDERSTOOD VERB = NOMINATIVE CASE

EXAMPLE: Jane is taller than I.

HINT: Mentally finish the sentence in elliptical constructions.

           Jane is taller than I am.

OBJECT OF PREPOSITION = OBJECTIVE CASE

EXAMPLE: Between you and me, I think he's wrong.

SUBJECT COMPLEMENT (AFTER BE VERB) = NOMINATIVE CASE

EXAMPLE: It was she.

WHO AND WHOM BEGINNING DEPENDENT CLAUSES

The case of the pronoun beginning a subordinate clause is determined by its use in the clause which it begins. The case is not influenced by words outside the clause.

In order to analyze the (who, whom) problem, follow these steps:

STEP 1.   Pick out the subordinate clause.

STEP 2.   Determine how the pronoun is used in the clause (subject, subject complement, object of verb, object of preposition), and then decide according to the usual rules for pronoun usage.

PROBLEM: The new teacher (who, whom) has taken Mr. Collin's position came from the South.

STEP 1:   subordinate clause = (who, whom) has taken Mr. Collin's position

STEP 2:   In this clause the pronoun is the subject of the verb has taken; therefore, the nominative or subjective case of the pronoun is needed.

SOLUTION: The new teacher who has taken Mr. Collin's position came from the South.

PROBLEM:	Does anyone know (who, whom) the new teacher is?
STEP 1:	Subordinate clause = (who, whom) the new teacher is
STEP 2:	In the clause, <u>teacher</u> is the subject of <u>is</u>; the pronoun is a subject complement following the <u>be</u> verb. The nominative or subjective case is necessary.
SOLUTION:	Does anyone know <u>who</u> the new teacher is?

NOTE: In determining whether to use <u>who</u> or <u>whom</u>, do not be misled by a parenthetical expression like <u>I</u> <u>think</u> or <u>he said</u>.

EXAMPLE: They are the people <u>who</u>, I think, are the foundations of society.

SOME ADDITIONAL RULES TO REMEMBER ABOUT PRONOUNS

RULE #1	**<u>Anyone</u>, <u>everyone</u>, <u>someone</u>, <u>everybody</u>, <u>somebody</u>, <u>anybody</u> and <u>nobody</u> (indefinite pronouns) are singular. The singular pronoun <u>his</u> is used with them.**
EXAMPLE:	<u>Anyone</u> may submit <u>his</u> name for consideration.

RULE # 2	**Avoid double subjects and useless pronouns.**
INCORRECT:	<u>Frank</u> <u>he</u> likes television.
	In <u>Huck Finn</u> <u>it</u> tells about a journey down the Mississippi.
CORRECT:	<u>Frank</u> likes television.
	<u>Huck Finn</u> tells about a journey down the Mississippi.

RULE #3	**When a pronoun modifies a gerund (a verbal noun), it is used as an adjective and is in the possessive case.**
INCORRECT:	He objected to me leaving.
CORRECT:	He objected to <u>my</u> <u>leaving</u>.

↓

Possessive Gerund Pronoun

RULE #4	**Never use <u>hisself</u> or <u>theirself</u>, use <u>himself</u> or <u>themselves</u>.**

PRONOUN PRACTICE

DIRECTIONS: Choose the correct pronoun for each sentence. Carefully review the explanatory answers when you are finished.

1.   I am not certain that (yours, your's) is the best solution.

2.   Our club sent two delegates, Ruth and (I, me), to the convention.

3.   In the first row of the orchestra sat Robert and (he, him).

4.   Sean knows his grammar lesson better than (him, he).

5.   (We, Us) two girls have been friends for a long time.

6.   The group consisted of John, Henry, and (I, me).

7.   This is Sam, (who, whom), I am sure, will be glad to serve you.

8.   (Who, Whom) shall we invite?

9.   Mother disapproves of (me, my) staying out late.

10.   It was (we, us) girls who won the contest.

ANSWERS:

1. yours   Do not confuse the possessive pronoun with a contraction. Your's would stand for your is.

2. me   Pronouns in apposition (renaming a noun) are the same case as the noun. Delegates is the object of the verb sent so we need the objective pronoun me.

3. he   He is the subject of this inverted order sentence.

4. he   Elliptical - "better than he knows it."

5. We   Subject - We have been friends.

6. me   Object of the preposition of.

7. who   "Who will be glad to serve you." Who is the subject of will be.

8. whom   We shall invite whom? Whom is the object of the verb invite.

9. my   A possessive pronoun is used before an ing word acting as a noun. (The ing word is called a gerund.)

10. we   Was is a form of to be. It is always followed by the nominative form in formal English. (The forms of be are - am, are, is, was, were, be, being, been.)

How did you do? Remember to study the areas in which you are still having difficulty.

C. VERBS

You must know the principal parts of important irregular verbs in order to speak good English.

The principal parts of any verb are as follows:

1. The present tense (I break.)

2. The past tense (I broke.)

3. The past participle (I have broken.) This is the form used with a helping verb such as <u>am</u>, <u>is</u>, <u>has</u>, <u>have</u>, <u>had</u>, etc. One of the most common errors is to use the past tense where you need the past participle or vice versa.

EXAMPLE: The dish was <u>broke</u>.

With <u>was</u> you need the past participle <u>broken</u>.

CORRECT: The dish <u>was</u> <u>broken</u>.

EXAMPLE: I <u>seen</u> him.

There is no helper here, so you need the simple past <u>saw</u>.

CORRECT: I <u>saw</u> him.

Here are the principal parts of some commonly used irregular verbs. As you read them try to think of the drill

Today I _____ Yesterday I ___ I have _____

as you read each principal part. Star the ones you have trouble with and **make sure you memorize them.**

PRESENT	PAST	PAST PARTICIPLE
Arise	Arose	have arisen
Bear	Bore	have borne
Beat	Beat	have beaten
Become	Became	have become
Begin	Began	have begun
Bend	Bent	have bent
Bite	Bit	have bitten
Blow	Blew	have blown
Break	Broke	have broken
Bring	Brought	have brought
Burst	Burst	have burst
Catch	Caught	have caught
Choose	Chose	have chosen
Come	Came	have come
Creep	Crept	have crept
Dig	Dug	have dug
Dive	Dived	have dived
Do	Did	have done
Draw	Drew	have drawn
Drink	Drank	have drunk
Drive	Drove	have driven
Drown	Drowned	have drowned
Eat	Ate	have eaten
Fall	Fell	have fallen
Flee	Fled	have fled
Fling	Flung	have flung
Fly	Flew	have flown
Forget	Forgot	have forgotten
Freeze	Froze	have frozen
Get	Got	have got or gotten
Give	Gave	have given
Go	Went	have gone
Grow	Grew	have grown
Hide	Hid	have hidden

PRESENT	PAST	PAST PARTICIPLE
Hurt	Hurt	have hurt
Kneel	Knelt	have knelt
Know	Knew	have known
Lay	Laid	have laid
Lead	Led	have led
Lend	Lent	have lent
Lie	Lay	have lain
Lose	Lost	have lost
Ride	Rode	have ridden
Ring	Rang	have rung
Rise	Rose	have risen
Run	Ran	have run
Say	Said	have said
See	Saw	have seen
Set	Set	have set
Shake	Shook	have shaken
Shine	Shone	have shone
Shrink	Shrank	have shrunk
Sing	Sang	have sung
Sink	Sank	have sunk
Sit	Sat	have sat
Slay	Slew	have slain
Speak	Spoke	have spoken
Spring	Sprang or sprung	have sprung
Steal	Stole	have stolen
Strike	Struck	have struck
Sting	Stung	have stung
Swear	Swore	have sworn
Sweep	Swept	have swept
Swim	Swam	have swum
Swing	Swung	have swung
Take	Took	have taken
Tear	Tore	have torn
Throw	Threw	have thrown
Wear	Wore	have worn
Wring	Wrung	have wrung
Write	Wrote	have written

TROUBLESOME VERB PAIR: LIE AND LAY

Most people do not use these verbs correctly. Only by taking time to think through each form you use, will you be able to establish the habit of using these verbs correctly.

STEP #1 Memorize the principal parts and meaning of each verb.

	PRESENT	PRESENT PARTICIPLE	PAST	PAST PARTICIPLE
Lie (rest or recline)	is lying	lay	have lain
Lay (to put or place)	is laying	laid	have laid

STEP #2 When faced with a lie-lay problem ask yourself two questions:

QUESTION 1: What is the meaning that I intend? Is it to be in a lying position or to put something down?

QUESTION 2: What is the time expressed by the verb and what principal part is needed to express this time?

EXAMPLE: After the alarm had awakened me, I (lay, laid) in bed too long and was late for work.

QUESTION 1: The meaning needed is to rest in bed.

The verb needed is lie.

QUESTION 2: The time is past and requires the past form. If you have done your memorizing work, you know that this is lay.

SOLUTION: After the alarm had awakened me, I lay in bed too long and was late for work.

EXAMPLE: The player has (lain, laid) his cards on the table.

QUESTION 1: The meaning needed is <u>put</u> or <u>placed</u>. The verb needed is <u>lay</u>.

QUESTION 2: The time is <u>past</u> and there is a helping verb. The past participle is needed and that is <u>laid</u>.

SOLUTION: The player has <u>laid</u> all his cards on the table.

SOME RULES TO REMEMBER ABOUT VERBS

RULE #1   **<u>Of</u> is not a substitute for <u>have</u> or <u>'ve</u>.**

INCORRECT: I could of cried.

CORRECT: I could have cried.

RULE #2.   **<u>Ought</u> is not preceded by <u>have</u> or <u>had</u>.**

INCORRECT: You had ought to buy the car now.

CORRECT: You ought to buy the car now.

RULE #3   **<u>Would</u> or <u>should</u> forms of the verb are not used in <u>if</u> clauses.**

INCORRECT: If we would have gone we might have seen him.

CORRECT: If we had gone we might have met.

RULE #4   **Use the present subjunctive form in an <u>if</u> clause of a statement that is obviously not true. This is called a condition contrary to fact. The verb most frequently involved is <u>to be</u>. The present of <u>to be</u> in the subjunctive is <u>were</u>.**

EXAMPLE: If I were you, I would not go. (I am not you).

161

D. VERBALS

Verbals are verb forms used as other parts of speech. The three verbals are the **infinitive**, the **gerund**, and the **participle**.

1. The **infinitive** is usually preceded by <u>to</u>:   It is used as a noun, adjective or adverb. It can never be the main verb of the sentence.

    It is not fair <u>to cheat</u>.

2. The **participle** is used as an adjective. The present participle ends in <u>ing</u>. Past participles have several endings (<u>ed</u>, <u>d</u>, <u>t</u>, <u>n</u>, <u>en</u>)

    The <u>dripping</u> water annoyed me.

    I love freshly <u>fallen</u> snow.

3. The **gerund** is the <u>ing</u> form used as a noun.

    <u>Running</u> has become very popular recently.

PRACTICE USING IRREGULAR VERBS

DIRECTIONS: Some of the sentences below are correct. Some have incorrect forms of verbs. Cross out the incorrect forms and replace them with the correct ones.

1. The boys have broke the window.

2. You should have chose Jimmy.

3. We had drunk all the punch.

4. I had flew to California.

5. All of us were nearly froze.

6. The dam had bursted.

7. I had lain in bed all morning.

8. Tell Rover to lay down.

9. I had gone to the store earlier.

10. Has she rang the bell?

11. You might have fallen on your head.

12. You must have stole my pencil.

13. She had tore her new dress.

14. I laid the book on the table.

15. She brang her book to class.

ANSWERS:

1. broken   past participle needed after <u>have</u>

2. chosen   past participle needed after <u>have</u>

3. Correct

4. flown   past participle needed after <u>had</u>

5. frozen   past participle needed with <u>were</u>

6. burst   <u>burst</u> does not change in form

7. Correct

8. lie   meaning = rest

9. Correct

10. rung   past participle needed after <u>had</u>

11. Correct

12. stolen   need past participle after <u>had</u>

13. torn   need past participle after <u>had</u>

14. Correct

15. brought   past of bring is <u>brought</u>

E. ADJECTIVES AND ADVERBS

Adjectives have three degrees of comparison:

POSITIVE: expressing a quality - as <u>short</u> or <u>fat</u>.

COMPARATIVE: used to speak of <u>two</u> persons or things - as <u>shorter</u> or <u>fatter</u>.

SUPERLATIVE: expressing the highest degree used to speak of three or more persons or things - as <u>shortest</u> or <u>fattest</u>.

Comparisons of adjectives that are long or would be hard to pronounce with <u>er</u> and <u>est</u> are made by using <u>more</u> and <u>most</u>.

EXAMPLE: more beautiful   most beautiful

more gracious   most gracious

Some adjectives are compared irregularly.

EXAMPLE: good   better   best

bad   worse   worst

Do not use double comparisons.

INCORRECTLY: My grades are <u>more higher</u> than yours.

CORRECT: My grades are higher than yours.

Do not compare adjectives that are absolutes.

EXAMPLE: <u>round</u>, <u>perfect</u>, <u>unique</u>, <u>final</u>, <u>mortal</u>.

The same general principles apply to the comparison of adverbs.

EXAMPLE: gracefully   more gracefully   most gracefully

fast   faster   fastest

badly   worse   worst

SOME ADDITIONAL RULES TO REMEMBER
ABOUT ADJECTIVES AND ADVERBS

RULE #1 After linking verbs such as <u>look</u>, <u>seem</u>, <u>appear</u>, <u>taste</u>, <u>smell</u>, <u>feel</u>, <u>sound</u>, use <u>adjectives</u> to describe the subject.

I feel bad. (not <u>badly</u>)

The food tastes good. (not <u>well</u>)

RULE #2 <u>Really</u> is an adverb; <u>real</u> is an adjective. Do not use <u>real</u> to modify another adjective.

INCORRECT: He's a real nice person.

CORRECT: He's a really nice person.

RULE #3 Adjectives do not modify verbs.

INCORRECT: Do what I say quick.

CORRECT: Do what I say quickly.

RULE #4 <u>Good</u> is never an adverb.

INCORRECT: The team played good.

CORRECT: The team played well.

RULE #5 Since <u>scarcely</u> and <u>hardly</u> are negative already, they should not be accompanied by another negative.

INCORRECT: I can't hardly see you.

CORRECT: I can hardly see you.

RULE #6 <u>Irregardless</u> is <u>not</u> a word. Use regardless.

F. PREPOSITIONS

A preposition is used to join a noun or pronoun to the rest of the sentence.

The following is a list of words commonly used as prepositions:

about	by	of	toward
above	concerning	off	under
across	down	on	underneath
after	during	over	until
at	except	past	up
before	for	since	upon
beneath	from	through	with
beside	in	throughout	within
but	into	to	without

The noun or pronoun following or dependent upon the preposition is called the object of the preposition.

RULES TO REMEMBER ABOUT PREPOSITIONS

RULE #1   **Generally, a sentence should not end with a preposition. However, you may end a sentence with a preposition if it will make the sentence smoother:**

AWKWARD: Did you really guess about what he was complaining?

BETTER: Did you really guess what he was complaining about?

RULE #2   **Avoid unnecessary prepositions.**

INCORRECT: Where is it at?

CORRECT: Where is it?

RULE #3   <u>Between</u> refers to two persons, groups, or things; <u>among</u> refers to more than two.

        EXAMPLE: Divide the money <u>among</u> the players.

        EXAMPLE: Divide the candy <u>between</u> yourself and Ann.

RULE #4   Use <u>because of</u> not <u>due to</u> to introduce a phrase.

        INCORRECT: <u>Due to</u> construction, traffic was delayed.

        CORRECT: <u>Because of</u> construction, traffic was delayed.

RULE #5   Do not use <u>off of</u> in place of <u>from</u> or <u>off</u>.

        INCORRECT: He got the present <u>off of</u> me.

                        Take your hands <u>off of</u> my dog.

        CORRECT: He got the present <u>from</u> me.

                        Take your hands <u>off</u> my dog.

RULE #6   <u>Into</u>, not <u>in</u>, implies going within.

"He walked in the house" means that while he was in the house he walked.

"He walked into the house" means that he walked from the outside into the house.

G. CONJUNCTIONS

A conjunction joins words or groups of words.

COORDINATING CONJUNCTIONS: join units or words of equal value. The most common are <u>and</u>, <u>but</u>, <u>or</u>, <u>nor</u>, <u>for</u>.

CORRELATIVE CONJUNCTIONS: are pairs of conjunctions that join similar elements in the same sentence. The most common are <u>either - or</u>, <u>neither - nor</u>, <u>both - and</u>, <u>not only - but also</u>.

SUBORDINATING CONJUNCTIONS: make one group of words dependent on another group. Some common ones are <u>when</u>, <u>because</u>, <u>if</u>, <u>since</u>, <u>although</u>, <u>while</u>.

RULES TO REMEMBER ABOUT CONJUNCTIONS

RULE #1 Use <u>since</u> or <u>because</u> instead of <u>being</u> or <u>being that</u> or <u>seeing as how</u> to introduce a clause.

INCORRECT: <u>Being that</u> you are tired, you may leave early.

CORRECT: <u>Since</u> you are tired, you may leave early.

RULE #2 Use <u>as</u>, not <u>like</u>, as a connective between clauses.

INCORRECT: He decided to do <u>like</u> he pleased.

CORRECT: He decided to do <u>as</u> he pleased.

RULE #3 <u>While</u> means "duration of time." It cannot be used in place of <u>but</u>, <u>although</u>, or <u>and</u>.

> INCORRECT: I like mushrooms <u>while</u> Don dislikes them intensely.

> CORRECT: I like mushrooms, <u>but</u> Don dislikes them intensely.

RULE #4 Do not say "the reason is because." Use "the reason is."

RULE #5 Do not say "the place is where." Use "the place is."

PRACTICE WITH MODIFIERS, PREPOSITIONS AND CONJUNCTIONS

1. Of Mary and her sister, Mary was the (prettiest, prettier).

2. Sue had just received the (worse, worst) report card of her life.

3. I envy the (most tallest, tallest) person in the class.

4. They should (of, 've) waited for us.

5. (Because of, Due to) the water shortage, we could not fill our pool.

6. That man runs (good, well).

7. Please do (like, as) I say.

8. The reason I am late is (because, that) traffic was heavy.

9. Get that snake (off of, off) my desk.

10. That painting is (unique, most unique).

ANSWERS:

1. prettier   Use the comparative form when speaking of two people

2. worst Use   the superlative form when speaking of three or more instances.

3. tallest   Most tallest is an incorrect form.

4. 've   The contraction 've for have is needed.

5. Because of   Due to is ungrammatical.

6. well   The adverb well is needed to modify the verb runs.

7. as   The conjunction as, not the preposition like, is needed to introduce a dependent clause.

8. that   Reason is because is ungrammatical.

9. off   Off of is ungrammatical.

10. unique   Unique means "one of a kind." It cannot be compared.